REAL PEOPLE,

REAL CRISES

REAL PEOPLE REAL CRISES:

An Inside Look at Corporate Crisis Communications

STEVE WILSON

Foreword by Luke Feck

OAKHILL PRESS
WINCHESTER, VA

10   9   8   7   6   5   4   3   2   1

Cover design: Michael Komarck

Interior design: Craig Hines

Original cartoon illustrations: Cyndi Bellerose

Library of Congress Cataloging-in-Publication Data

Wilson, Steve, 1946–
    Real people, real crisis : an inside look at corporate crisis communications / Steve Wilson.
        p. cm.
    Includes index.
    ISBN 1-886939-52-7
    1. Crisis management. 2. Corporations—Public relations. I. Title.

HD49 .W55 2002
658.4'056—dc21   2002072260

CONTENTS

CONTENTS

FOREWORD

By Luke Feck

Senior Vice President/Corporate Communications (Retired)
American Electric Power

Former editor of *The Cincinnati Enquirer* and *The Columbus Dispatch*

I f you think "nuggets" are for gold prospectors and "bridges" for civil engineers, read on. Steve Wilson can add new dimensions to those words.

Originally a crisis was the time when a truly sick person took a decisive turn for life or death. The word is used in astrology when the planets align in a way that affects the flow of events.

But you and I know it is a time when the sirens sound, the phones ring and the pagers throb. Something has gone wrong. It needs to be understood, explained and fixed. That's where Steve Wilson comes in, preferably before the ringing and the throbbing but often somewhere along in the process.

I met Steve when he worked for a genial but tough state editor at *The Cincinnati Enquirer* in the early 1970s. He was our Indiana correspondent and in time became our political writer. By the time he was in Columbus as our bureau chief covering state government, the *Enquirer* was being sold to the Gannett Company. *USA Today* was a gleam in the eye of Gannett's management. Soon enough *USA Today* began plucking talented staffers from their papers and placing them on the staff of the fledging national daily newspaper. Steve became Chicago correspondent responsible for the Midwest. He was still the one on the phone asking the hard questions of companies or politicians but for a national audience.

When it came time for a career change, Steve could simply put himself on the other side of the desk and help people answer the tough questions, the questions he had been asking all his life. He knew from experience how a focused response could change the tone of a story, how a nuance can lead a reporter to a deeper level of understanding an issue.

He also knew that there were many respondents woefully unprepared for that ring of the phone. They are smart with pedigreed skill sets but they wilt when a microphone is stuck in their mouth or a camera unblinkingly stares into their soul. A career was born and a course set.

Recently I read Bernard Goldberg's *Bias* and I watch, on occasion, Bill O'Reilly in his *No Spin Zone*. Bias and spin, while not new words, have been much on people's minds. Do reporters really have inherent biases? Are they anti-business? Do politicians spin every possible story their way? Or do they turn every event into a negative for "the other side?" What is a chemical plant manager supposed to do when suddenly he is thrust into a situation where everyone seems to be playing by rules he neither knows nor understands?

If you are involved in a crisis, you don't have time for spin or bias. You and your company, your hospital, your municipality have a stake in the story, or you wouldn't be there. Your job is to tell your side of the story as factually as you can in a way that will be best understood by your audiences. There are as many audiences as there are different events. It can be an audience of your employees, your boss, neighbors around your facility, people in your community, your shareholders, the wire services, newspaper readers, television viewers—or a composite.

Pay close attention the next time you see someone on television speaking on behalf of a company in crisis. Is she believable? Is he prepared? What are the points she wants to make? Does he make them? This book can help you if you were suddenly quaking in their shoes.

The job, simply, is to determine what is to be said (the nuggets) and how to get back to those nuggets (the bridge) when questions are asked. That's what Steve Wilson teaches based on his experience as a reporter and a trainer. Even though you may never be comfortable in a crisis, you can be competent, effective and unflappable in getting your story out just the way you want it. That's what it's all about.

INTRODUCTION

W hen I first started to take on this endeavor, it was supposed to be a textbook on crisis management, or at least a "how to" book.

It didn't turn out that way.

It became a documentary of sorts on dealing with very real crises, and *preparing* to deal with them. It became an extension of our workshops on media training and crisis management where students never seemed to tire of hearing how real people— just like themselves—dealt with the crises that life throws at them. It became a collection of anecdotes, personal thoughts, and observations from a career in both journalism and crisis management.

Rather than second-guess how someone else handled a crisis, I wanted to deal with crises I was personally involved in. I decided to use my own case studies, not ones I had only read about. I wanted to write about them the way they happened. To the degree possible, I have tried to do that. Fortunately, I have thousands of pages of reports, news releases, letters, speeches, and magazine articles I've written over the years that have helped keep me on track.

Since much of the work we do is of a confidential nature, I have altered names, locations, and circumstances in some cases to protect our clients. I have not, however, altered the nature of the crises or how they were addressed. The events portrayed are not fiction. They did happen.

In some instances, I have tried to re-create dialogue from real-life situations. That dialogue is often based on videotapes, notes, or other documentation. In some cases, the dialogue is verbatim. In some cases, it is based on my best recollection. The dialogue and thoughts in the opening chapter are based on literally hundreds of conversations with students and my attempt to place myself in their shoes under the circumstances. I wanted people to know what my students voluntarily subject themselves to in order to better combat crises.

My endeavor was not to present the ultimate guide for crisis management, but to let readers know how others have dealt with real crises in a real world. As with our workshops, I didn't want to lecture people, but to let them draw their own conclusions based on their experiences and the experiences of others.

PROLOGUE

NEVER SAY NEVER

If a single event in world history ever demonstrated the need for being prepared for the unexpected, it was the tragedy that became America's nightmare the morning of September 11, 2001.

It's one of those rare events in history where everyone will always remember exactly where they were and what they were doing at the exact time they found out about it. You couldn't erase it from your memory if you wanted to.

My wife Donna and I were at a nuclear facility in the Ohio Valley that morning attending a briefing for a scheduled mock disaster that was to begin the next morning. The exercise was to be a realistic test of the facility's crisis management and emergency response capabilities. It had been more than six months in development and would involve literally scores of players and impact scores of others. The test was to be graded by The Nuclear Regulatory Commission.

There were about 50 of us in the briefing room going over the minute details of the drill when telephones and pagers began sounding and vibrating. After more than a half-dozen security personnel had excused themselves from our briefing, we knew something serious was happening.

Most of us—without radios or cell phones in a closed briefing room—had no idea of what was going on. Then a paramedic interrupted the briefing to tell us that a plane or planes had just crashed into the World Trade Center and another had crashed into the Pentagon. There was a quick sigh and then silence as we tried to comprehend what would become America's newest war. The meeting's facilitator tried to continue, but within a few moments it was apparent that continuing would be impossible. No one was thinking about the mock disaster that was supposed to take place tomorrow. We were thinking about the real disaster that was unfolding today.

At that moment, our crisis drill seemed rather insignificant. We were trying to prepare for what we felt was a realistic crisis only to find out that reality was far more cruel than anything any of us could ever envision. We looked at each other. We were speechless. None of us knew what to do. I talked to a lady next to me and we both shared our inner thoughts about what we were feeling at that time. I had never met her before. I don't know her name and I'll probably never see her again. But, at that moment, she and I and everyone in that room bonded. We were experiencing a horrible event in world history and we were experiencing it together. I'm sure the same thing was going on around the United States and around the world. As a reporter, I had covered shootings, bombings, plane crashes, and even a war. As a crisis management specialist, I'd seen the dark side of mankind. But nothing I had done in my life had prepared me for what happened that day. Nothing could.

I remember the drive home that day. Planes weren't flying. My cellphone rang a few times. My associates who were to be participating in the next day's mock disaster wanted to know if it had been canceled. They already knew the answer. I think they just wanted to talk to someone. These were all seasoned reporters. They had seen everything. They had covered everything. But today, they were as dumbfounded as the rest of us.

Since that date, I have been asked by reporters, clients, and others what corporations and organizations could do to prepare for such a catastrophe. I've been asked what countries can do to prepare for such an event. I'm not sure I have ever found an acceptable answer to the question. I'm not sure one exists.

I was at another nuclear facility years earlier and suggested a training scenario in which an airplane intentionally crashed into the compound. It was one of those "War of the Worlds" scenarios I come up with from time to time. I was told it was too outlandish, that it could never happen. The idea was killed in favor of a more "credible" scenario.

What happened on September 11, 2001, tells us to never say "never." We now know that the impossible not only can happen, it did

September 11 also warns us that we have to take precautions to prepare and protect our organizations and our people from the "worst-case scenarios" that might be far-fetched, as well as the lesser nightmares that are far more likely to happen.

> We have to be able to communicate openly and honestly with our employees, customers, the news media, and the public—even when our own world seems to have come to an end.

We know now that we have to be able to operate even if we don't have offices, equipment, records, or key executives. We have to be able to communicate openly and honestly with our employees, customers, the news media, and the public—even when our own world seems to have come to an end.

I used to say we might not be able to prevent all crises, but at least we can be prepared to deal with them. Since

September 11, 2001, that task has become tougher, but it still has to be the goal. We have to at least try.

Businesses can no longer place crisis management plans and crisis training on a back burner. Dealing with potential crises has to be given a higher priority—and throughout a growing segment of corporations and organizations, it is. You don't have to be General Motors to need a crisis plan. Crises are nondiscriminatory. They could care less how big or small you are.

Training in realistic scenarios and regular drilling is a must.

Reading a book, watching a video, or listening to a lecture isn't enough. You have to get involved. You can't wait to experience the real thing. The cost is too high.

GETTING READY

It wasn't the biggest fire in the city's history, but there were flames and fire engines. And, of course, there were reporters to cover all of it on live televsion

The fire had taken place near the runway on a busy Monday morning, forcing the closure and evacuation of the airport. Traffic was halted on the interstate and the only thing hotter than the flames rising from the giant fuel tanks were the tempers of commuters who were going to miss their planes and the thousands of motorists stuck in the three-mile-long parking lot that used to be Interstate 44.

There, in the midst of all the news media commotion, was an executive with the company that owned the flaming fuel tanks. He was his organization's "corporate spokesperson," and his job was to talk with reporters. He was visibly nervous. Clearly he'd rather be somewhere else, anywhere else than in front of the television camera.

"How did it happen?" the reporter asked.

It wasn't really a tough question, but he had no idea at this time about how or why, and especially why now?

"Why weren't you able to prevent it?"

Now the reporter had crossed the line, he felt. The interview was already becoming accusatory and it had barely started.

"What do you mean?" he thought silently. "Like I could have prevented it? I just let it happen? It wasn't something

Conducting a news media interview in a crisis can be frightening, but it's a lot easier if you're prepared for it.

I knew was going to happen. How the heck could I have prevented it? Now that's really a stupid question!"

"How toxic is the smoke?" the reporter asked, his eyes glaring directly into the executive's.

"What do you mean? You idiot," he thought. "We're talking about aviation fuel, not some toxic chemicals. Any fool knows that. Where did this guy come from?"

The light perched atop the television camera seemed brighter than the midday sun and it felt like it was just inches from his forehead. He could feel the heat from it. The microphone appeared more like a weapon than a tool of journalism. He was beginning to sweat.

"How many people were injured?" the reporter asked.

"Nobody said anyone was injured," he thought to himself. "No one told me. Where did you find that out? Can people see my knees shaking?"

"What are you doing for them?" the next question came out of nowhere.

"What do you mean?" he thought to himself. "What are we doing for them? We didn't even know anyone was injured. God, this is bad, I had no idea it was this bad. I just thought we had a fire. That's bad enough."

"Could the situation get worse?" the reporter asked, his microphone thrust right below the spokesperson's nose.

"What do you mean? Of course it could get worse," he thought, knowing far too well how bad it could have been. "It could get a lot worse. That's what we're trying to prevent, you piranha. Where on Earth did you come up with a question like that anyway? Is that what they teach you in journalism school?"

He knew what he needed to say, but the words would not come out. They were stuck somewhere between his brain and his throat, and at the moment, his brain apparently had abandoned him. It was as if it were lying on the ground in front of him, looking back up at him as if to say, "You're on your own now, buddy!"

There in front of the TV camera and a gathering throng of onlookers, he had never felt so alone in his life. Nor, perhaps, as scared.

He knew if he said the wrong thing, it would only make matters worse. And that was certainly something he didn't need. Things were bad enough as it was.

> There in front of the TV camera and a gathering throng of onlookers, he had never felt so alone in his life. Nor, perhaps, as scared.

Now what was it he was supposed to say? Something about being in control of the situation, that was it! Sure, he was in control of the situation. He could almost feel the heat from the flames as he began to talk to the reporter.

"Who's going to believe me? I think I'm going to be sick," he thought. "What's it going to look like throwing up on live television?

"Why did I agree to do this anyway? Why is this man trying to trick me? Why doesn't he just shut up and let me answer his question? He seemed so nice before . . . before the camera was on and before the questions began. God, I've never done an interview with a reporter before. Why now? It never looked like this on television. What do they know that I don't?

"Okay, I know I have to do something. I have to say something. I can't just stand here forever. How long has it been, anyway? It seems like hours. He's going to think I'm the dumbest person in the world. And, what about those people who are going to see this on television? Oh, why can't I just say something?"

What seemed like an eternity had only been a few seconds. And when he began to speak, the words came from . . . somewhere.

"Obviously, we have a serious situation on our hands right now," he said in his own homespun style, trying to remain as calm as possible under the circumstances. He established eye contact with the reporter, talking to him directly as he continued, "and our primary concern right now is to bring things under control as quickly as possible and assure the safety of those people in the affected area."

"What did I just say?" he tried to recall in his mind. He couldn't remember. It was like someone else was talking. It was an out-of-mind experience. He was out of his mind to get involved in this interview. He was convinced he had just failed his first interview on live television.

Even if he had said the right thing, who would believe him? Did it sound like he had memorized it? Did it sound canned? Was it just more corporate sound bites? He was already dreading the question the reporter would ask next.

"Why did I ever take this job?" he asked himself silently. "So this is what it's like to kiss off 25 years with the company," he thought.

And to think the whole thing was at least partially his idea.

What would his colleagues think? Were they going to think he was a jerk? "Who cares what they think? I just want to be out of here!"

What about his colleagues? Yes, what about his colleagues? They were all there in the adjoining room, going over their notes, trying to make conversation with one another and yet as nervous as anyone who has ever stood up before television cameras and tried to get their message across in the middle of a potential public relations crisis. Their time too was coming up, and they knew it. In just a few minutes, it would be their turn. They would be the ones trying to answer the reporters' questions.

But now, as they prepared for their day before the media, they were going over their message points one last time. They were reviewing what it was they would tell the reporter, and they were sweating.

They were awaiting their turn at facing the television

camera in this day-long course on dealing with the news media during a crisis. It was nothing more than a corporate-sponsored "media training" session. But it was so realistic, far more realistic than they thought it would be.

The eight executives were all there from the same company. It was a hotel conference center, not a busy airport. It was the middle of the week, not Monday rush hour. It was a session where executives would learn the do's and don'ts of dealing with reporters in a crisis. They were there to learn how to get their message across.

It was all part of a training session.

It was all fake, but the scenario was very realistic.

He had been one of the ones who had developed it. But still, it was just a scenario. It didn't really happen, although it could have. And, for those few minutes in front of the camera, his heart almost beating out of his chest, it was almost *too* real.

Later, they would play back the tapes and he and his colleagues would have a good laugh at each other. A nervous laugh. They would applaud when one of their comrades provided a quotable sound bite. They would gasp in horror when they saw an expression on their face when they heard a question they had never anticipated. They would ask, "Gosh, am I that fat? Do I really sound like that?"

Sure, they would be embarrassed. Sure, they would look kind of stupid once in a while. But they were not alone. They had plenty of company. And they were learning.

They were learning what it was like to talk to reporters during a crisis. They were learning that they had to stay focused. They had to stay *"on message."* And they were learning that there was nothing easy about it.

They were all top-level executives, or on their way to becoming one. They knew that if the make-believe scenario they faced today *really* happened, they would be the ones in front of the television cameras and in front of the public to tell them what happened, what caused it, and what they were doing about it. They hadn't studied these skills in college. It was not the kind of thing you could learn from a book or watching a videotape or listening to a speech. They knew in order to be good at it, they had to do it. They had to do it themselves.

That's why they took a precious few hours from their workweek to potentially humiliate themselves in front of their coworkers. That's why they worked up the courage to do something they had always dreaded. It was a humbling experience, a few of them would say later.

They were concerned that without this training, they would still have to face the cameras and microphones. They knew they could say the wrong thing and they knew they could make their company look bad on national television or on the front page of their local newspaper.

This test was not something they especially wanted to do. It was something they all knew too well that they needed to. They *had* to do it.

While their session was going on in Oklahoma City, similar sessions were going on in other cities across the country, and around the world.

Corporate America—and corporations from Great Britain to Japan—were learning how to take on the news media. They were learning how to deal with the media and the public when things don't especially go the way they should. They were hoping the training they were going through today would prevent the public relations disasters of tomorrow.

After his interview was over and he had some time to reflect on what he had done wrong, and what he had done right, the spokesman from Oklahoma City talked with his instructor and his colleagues over a ham and cheese sandwich. He asked if that was what reporters were *really* like. He asked if other people had made the same mistakes he had made that morning in front of the camera. He almost took a degree of relief to know they had. He was also pleased to learn that most people do better in real-life interviews than in practice sessions.

Later that day, he would go through a simulated news conference and more television interviews. He would learn about things like when and how to "bridge" a question and get to the core message. He would learn about eye contact and he would learn how to stay calm in the midst of a calamity.

And when the session was all over and he was exhausted both physically and mentally, he joined the others in his class in telling what he had learned from this day of confrontation.

"You know," he told the instructor and his classmates that day in his Oklahoma drawl, "after going through your workshop today, I know I'm still not ready for *60 Minutes*. But I do know this: if I have to deal with the news media in some real crisis situation, at least I won't step in it."

Everyone laughed. They knew exactly what he meant.

MAKING YOUR
OWN LUCK

When you think about crisis management, it's easy to turn to classics like Tylenol, the Exxon *Valdez*, Dow Corning, Perrier, Pepsi, or Firestone Tires.

Of course we remember them—for what they did right . . . or wrong. They have become textbook cases. They have become urban legends. They have become as much myth as reality. No one probably was ever as good as history remembers . . . or as bad. The stories seem to get exaggerated with age. The good get better, the bad get worse. With any real luck, they are forgotten.

The truth is that crises—or potential crises—happen every day to corporations and organizations all over the globe. Most of them—to the relief of those involved—are not well publicized.

They have been handled well . . . and not so well.

The truth is that you've probably never heard of most of America's worst crises. If the facts were ever revealed, you'd have a new appreciation for what really can go wrong in business, government, and industry. It can get pretty bad.

In some cases, the people involved in these potential crises of the modern day were lucky, but in the majority of cases, they were instrumental in making their own luck. Or, as one of those closely involved in what could have become a major international crisis said afterwards, "The more prepared I am, the luckier I get."

> The truth is that crises—or potential crises—happen every day to corporations and organizations all over the globe. Most of them—to the relief of those involved—are not well publicized.

Paul wasn't the first person to coin that phrase, I'm sure, but as a top executive with a Louisiana-based chemical company, he knew what he was talking about. I first met him in the late 1980s. It was right after his company had been featured in a series on the chemical industry.

Before the series had been written, Paul was under the impression that the newspaper was going to do a favorable story on the chemical industry in Louisiana and his company was to be one of the ones highlighted. At least that's what he recalled from his initial conversations with the paper. Paul was a trusting soul. He had no reason to doubt what they said.

Eventually the story ran and Paul's company was highlighted for sure, but the story was anything but favorable. He took it very personally.

He could have done what so many other executives have done when they've been burned in the news media. He could have stayed away from any future dealings with reporters. He could have taken the "no comment" approach. He could have hidden his head in the sand. Instead, he chose another avenue. He decided to prepare himself for the "next time." He wasn't sure when it would happen or what the issue would be, but he was convinced it was just a matter of time.

Over the next 18 months or so, he asked our firm to take his top managers through a series of training programs to enhance their communications skills with the news media and the public. We wrote a crisis plan for his organization and we helped them launch a community relations program. He was quite serious about doing whatever he could to enhance and protect his company's image.

Stories about his company appeared from time to time in the news media. Some were good. Others were not, but he never flinched at responding to reporters' inquiries. I'm convinced he felt it was his obligation, his duty.

Then came the time bomb. One of Paul's plants was being investigated for potential violations of federal environmental laws. The weeks turned into months as the investigation continued. We didn't know where it would go, but we knew it had the possibility to create a major public relations nightmare. Throughout the whole time, we worked on putting together a plan on how to deal with whatever might develop. We prepared for the worst.

When the story finally hit the media, our worst nightmare had come true. The potential fines and penalties were in a class by themselves. It appeared the government wanted to make an example of Paul's company. The story broke in Washington as well as Louisiana, but we were ready. We had made contacts with employees, shareholders, government and community leaders, as well as the news media. We knew where we stood on the issue and so did everyone else. The company believed in its position and it believed it had done the right thing.

At the end of what turned out to be a very long day of interviews with reporters from all over the country, Paul and I were discussing the day's activities and trying to figure out what would happen next. We talked about all of the work we had put into planning how we would deal with the problem. We talked about all the ways the situation could have turned out, and we were both rather pleased with the ultimate outcome. We both knew it could have been a lot worse. What Paul and his managers had done over the past year had taken a lot of time, effort, and money, but they were prepared to deal with just about anything that could have happened. From their perspective, it was well worth the trouble.

Preparation: the lifeblood of crisis management.

It was in the middle of a media training workshop in Wyoming a few years ago when the pager on my belt began vibrating. I was in the middle of telling my students about the importance of "staying on message," so I temporarily ignored it. Then it went off again a few seconds later. I looked at it. At the end of the number— my office number—was a 3-digit message: 9-1-1.

I called for an unplanned recess, excused myself, and grabbed my cell phone. I think the students understood the urgency of the situation. I like to think they'd want me to offer them the same consideration if the tables were turned and it was their emergency I was responding to. I called my office back in Ohio and my secretary gave me the number of a man in San Diego. He had given no real explanation other than to say it was "very important. I'd understand."

"Hi, Steve," he said upon answering. "You may not remember me, but I was in one of your workshops in Chicago about a year ago. Well, you gave me this card with your 800 number on it and you said to give you a call if we ever needed help. You got a few minutes? Not bothering you, am I?"

"Of course not," I told him, as I glanced down the hallway at the media training class, still in recess. My assistant was talking to them. She seemed to be handling it fine for the time being.

"Well, we've got something of an issue out here. It seems we had a problem with one of our products. Sort of like an explosion. . . . Well, really, it *was* an explosion. Not really a big one, understand, but I guess you can say it exploded. And, well, a local TV station did a story on it last night and now there's a TV crew out in our front lobby and I was just hoping. . . ."

That's the way the call came in—verbatim—as well as I can remember it. Unfortunately, that type of call is not an uncommon occurrence. The words vary, but the message is always the same. The barbarians are at the gate and those guarding the gate aren't sure at all how to deal with them.

When we conduct media training and crisis management training sessions around the country, I tell workshop participants about the importance of their first response. I tell them what they do and what they communicate during the first minutes or first hours of a crisis may well shape public opinion for hours, days, weeks, and possibly forever.

> When the stakes are as high as they are in a crisis, you really don't want to delegate important decisions that can impact your company's future, or your own.

I also tell them that it's quite likely, when that crisis takes place, that they may be on their own without the aid of a public relations department—or agency—to help them out. They could be in a situation where they have to determine on their own exactly what to communicate to the public—through reporters.

And even under the best of circumstances, they should have a handle on what needs to be done and what needs to be said. They should never be in a position where they have to be totally dependent on aides, departments, consultants, or agencies for advice. Those people can change and their expertise in how to handle crises can vary widely. When the stakes are as high as they are in a crisis, you really don't want to delegate important decisions that can impact your company's future, or your own.

That's why so many companies and organizations today are relegating more and more time to crisis management training. They realize it's a vital area of their business that is better learned through training workshops and drills than through costly personal experience.

They know it's better to spend time, effort, and money now on how to deal with a crisis that might never happen than to try to wing it under real-life circumstances. They know they need to make their own luck. It's just another insurance policy for them. Why take a chance?

In the spring of 2001, I received an unexpected call from one of our clients who had worked with us in various workshops and drills for a number of years. We had also worked side-by-side in real crisis situations. It was sort of a strange call. It was a serious call. It was all business.

They wanted to know if I was free at the moment and how fast I could be in Little Rock, Arkansas. They didn't say why. I didn't ask. It was clear from the tone of the caller's voice that it was important.

I quickly checked the airline schedule and figured I could be there by late afternoon, if I hurried. I quickly drove home to pack a suitcase and then sped to the airport to catch my plane. I was on my cell phone with my client when I noticed the police officer. I just pulled over and tried to find my driver's license. Of course, I was in a hurry. From his perspective, it wasn't a good excuse. It's just one of the hazards of being a crisis management consultant.

When I got to my hotel room in Little Rock a few hours later, the message light was blinking. I checked it out. The recording told me I'd be meeting with my client the first thing next morning. He still wasn't telling me what was wrong. He asked me a favor.

"On your way over here, keep your eyes open and tell me what you see," he said.

I cheated. Early the next morning, I went jogging from the hotel over to the plant and back. There were semi trucks literally everywhere. I was beginning to wonder what was going on.

As I walked into his office an hour or so later, Ed was on the phone with a reporter. He motioned me to sit down. I couldn't help but overhear his side of the conversation. It was clear something was wrong with the product they produced there and the reporter seemed to already know it. The conversation continued for a while. Ed remained calm. From his side of the phone line, it didn't sound that bad.

When he hung up on the reporter, he asked, "So, what did you see on the way over here?"

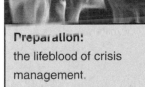

Preparation: the lifeblood of crisis management.

"A whole bunch of semi trucks," I said. "They were backed up on the street and lined up for what seemed a block or two. What's going on?"

"That noticeable, huh?" he grunted.

"Pretty hard to miss," I responded. "There's a lot of them."

"Well, let me tell you what's going on."

"I'd appreciate that," I replied.

"About three days ago, we got a call from one of our suppliers that they had detected higher-than-normal levels of a potentially dangerous chemical in one of the raw materials we use from them. Now, don't get excited just yet. There's more. We started checking it out and while the raw material did have accelerated levels of the chemical, the levels in the food product were still within acceptable limits under the FDA."

"But, I think you're telling me, those levels aren't acceptable to you . . . or your customers."

"Now you're on to it. Within a few hours after we found out about the problem, I got a call from a reporter in Nashville. She knew something was happening, but she had some bad information. She was asking about some poisonous chemical in our product. I was able to convince her there was no story.

"But then I got another call, the one you just heard, from a reporter in St. Louis, and he had a better hold on what was going on. Right now, I think we're just buying time."

From my standpoint, I told him, it sounded like they had already taken the right actions. All those trucks in front of the plant were hauling away the contaminated product and bringing in new product to replace it. It was a monstrous task, but they were making headway.

They had quietly "withdrawn" the product from the marketplace. There were no reports of anyone becoming ill, or even complaining. Consumer affairs had received no calls whatsoever.

But still, there were those two reporters who had some idea of what had happened. We just didn't know how much they knew. Even under the best of circumstances, consumers wouldn't like it. No one wants to think their food is contaminated with a chemical linked to cancer, even if the levels are possibly acceptable by the federal government. For most of us, there is no safe level of a chemical that can cause cancer. Any amount is too much.

Over the next few hours, the company recalled nearly all of the questionable food. It wasn't easy and it wasn't cheap. But they knew all too well that it needed to be done. It was being stored temporarily in a large warehouse where it ultimately would be hauled to a predesignated location for safe disposal.

Customers—those stores that sold the food—were being told that it did not meet the company's quality standards and, as a result, was being replaced. It was the truth. There was no mention of the chemical. No one asked.

The Food and Drug Administration (FDA) was contacted and told what we were doing. They agreed there was no health concern, but they totally understood the potential dilemma.

A media statement was being prepared, just in case:

> *"We were contacted last week by a supplier who told us there was a potential issue and that one of the ingredients did not fall within our quality standards and specifications. We contacted the Food and Drug Administration and it was determined there were no health concerns. However, since the product did not meet our own specifications for quality, we decided not to ship any potentially affected product."*

Like so many other media statements that are written and overly edited by committees, it sounded like the right thing to say at the time, I'm sure, but it wasn't written the way people really talk—at least not the way I talk, or the way Ed, our spokesperson, talks.

I suggested that perhaps we should have a shorter version that wouldn't sound so bureaucratic. We needed something that was more normal, something that didn't seem so canned. Reporters don't like canned statements. Neither does the public.

We came up with an abbreviated version:

> *"A problem was detected, it was handled promptly, and there was never any health concern."*

It was more like the sound bite reporters were looking for.

It sounded more like people talk. And we knew it would never be delivered exactly the way it was written anyway.

But Ed still needed to practice. He needed to be prepared for that tough question out of left field, that really *stupid* question or the question no one on our team would ever think of.

He had to be comfortable with what he would say. Reporters—good reporters at least—seem to have a sixth sense, almost a built-in lie detector that sends out an alarm when the person they're interviewing gets a little too nervous answering a question. In dealing with reporters, it's not just what you say, but how you say it. Would Ed be believable?

For Ed, it was vital that he had to believe what he was saying before he ever tried to make someone else believe him. As we went through a preliminary interview, I would break in occasionally and ask him: "Are you comfortable with that? Can you say that with full conviction? Because, Ed, if there is even a small doubt in your mind about it, we can change it. I don't want you telling the media anything you're not comfortable with."

We continued our practice session. Questions were asked . . . and answered out loud. Writing questions and potential answers down on a sheet of paper wouldn't be enough. He needed to hear the questions, not just read them. He had to answer the questions, out loud, not just say them in his mind. We wanted to make sure he didn't get caught by surprise. If there was a tough question out there, we wanted to make sure he heard it from us first, not some reporter. If he was going to get hung up on a question, I wanted to know now, not in the middle of a live television interview.

The company shared with the FDA what it was going to say. The crisis team didn't want them caught by surprise, should a reporter call them directly. Considering the circumstances, we thought that was quite probable. In return, the FDA gave us an idea of what they were saying. It was comforting. We were speaking off the same page. If this was going to become a major controversy, at least it wouldn't be between us and the FDA. There were enough others involved—or others who could become involved—to do that. They didn't need our help.

The crisis team now involved several dozen individuals who were spread over four metropolitan areas in four states. My first observation was that it resembled a military campaign—a very well-orchestrated military campaign. Out in the plant lot, dozens of semi trucks were loading up the contaminated product and bringing in new product. It was all being choreographed with exact precision. Inside the production area, yellow tape marked off areas where we needed to be cautious. If there was any confusion, it didn't show. There was probably less activity on the deck of an aircraft carrier, Ed remarked. There were literally hundreds of people on the job and it was clear they knew their job. No one was questioning what needed to be done. They were just doing what they knew they had to. They were working together. They were a team.

The very real scenario that was unfolding in Little Rock that day was not that different from some of the scenarios we had practiced together in crisis management training several times over the past several years. Many of those people involved in the operation, and all of those in key positions, had been participants in those training sessions. Somehow, it all seemed so far away then. While we all knew it was possible, it all seemed so unlikely. That was then. Now was now. It was all different today. Today, it was happening. And they were as ready as anyone could be ready to tackle a situation of this magnitude.

Because of the training and because of their crisis management plans, they knew what they needed to do . . . and they were doing it.

We were able to pro-act, as one employee would say, not simply react.

They had contemplated years before what could go wrong and what they would have to do to deal with it. They had identified who would play key parts in combating a crisis. They knew who would be their best spokesperson and they had some idea of what they would have to do . . . and say.

It was impossible for me to witness what was going on now without recalling those training drills of the past. But what was unfolding before our eyes that weekend in Little Rock was no drill. It was worse than anything we could envision. It was far worse than the scenario in our training.

Four days after it began, for the most part it was already over, with only minimal media coverage. The crisis that had the potential to cause so much destruction had been defused. It never exploded.

Why? It was apparent from the beginning. The company wasn't lucky. It had made its own luck. They had thought out what could go wrong and they had a plan on how to deal with it. Time and time again over the years, we had practiced how to deal with potential crisis situations. We had put together realistic scenarios—complete with television cameras and microphones—and we had dealt with them. We knew what could happen and we knew what we had to do. More importantly, we had a crisis team. And even the best crisis plan can't replace a well-organized and well-trained team.

You can learn from experiencing a crisis firsthand, but that can be costly and you most likely will learn as much or more from the mistakes you make than what you do right. Or, you can learn from realistic crisis scenarios in training. The mistakes still hurt, but they hurt a lot less than the ones you make in real life.

HOW TO
RECOGNIZE A CRISIS

I still remember a television reporter asking the question of a plant manager after an explosion: "Did you have any warning? Did you have any idea that something was about to go wrong?"

At the time, I thought it was just another dumb reporter question, not totally unlike the kind I used to ask back in the days when I was a reporter. Not every question you're asked by a reporter is a textbook question or the kind of question you'd think reporters would ask. Few, if any, reporters carry around a list of questions they want to ask. They act on instinct, training, and experience. Some questions don't make much sense to you at the time. That doesn't mean they don't make sense to the reporter, or to the public who might want to know the same thing.

"So what about it?" the reporter asked again. "Did you have any idea something was about to go wrong?"

At first, you might say, "Of course not. How can anyone predict a crisis?"

It's not like crises leave red flags all over the place to announce they are coming. Or do they?

Sometimes, there are indications that a crisis is coming. Sometimes, they do leave announcement cards, if you know where to look and know how to read them.

> Sometimes, there are indications that a crisis is coming. Sometimes, they do leave announcement cards, if you know where to look and know how to read them.

After spending a great many years covering crises as a reporter and working on them as a consultant, I can say honestly that while some crises come without any warning, some can be predicted, at least to a degree. If we're going to deal with them effectively, we must prepare for all kinds of crises—both those that can be predicted, as well as those that cannot.

That's why it's important to take the time *before* the crisis takes place to prepare for it. It's far more difficult once the crisis materializes.

So how exactly does one prepare for a crisis? For starters, you have to know what one is. You have to know you have a crisis if you expect to deal with it.

Not all crises are created equally. Some are a lot worse than others.

Some strike out of the blue, with little or no warning whatsoever. They explode. They burn. They can injure and even kill. They have short fuses and they burn quickly.

Some crises are slower burning. They can be that contaminated product you learned about this morning, the

Not all crises are alike. Some start off with a slow burn, while others can explode without warning.

layoff announcement planned for next week, or the potential class-action lawsuit that might be filed within the next few days.

In planning on how you might deal with crises, you first need to run an inventory of the potential crises that could impact you and your organization.

What could go wrong? What could happen? How would you react to it?

Those are the first questions you should ask yourself as you begin the task of how you would deal with a crisis situation.

Most people don't.

Unfortunately, they start off with the strategy of how they would react to a crisis without ever knowing what the crisis is, or what it involves. They jump all the way to "solution" without ever knowing the problem. They know what they are going to tell the public, long before they even know the details of what happened. That doesn't make a lot of sense. It's just plain wrong.

How would you like to stand in front of a building engulfed in flames and tell television reporters and the world that the situation is under control? Even if it's true, no one would believe you.

I remember the media training class many years ago, not long after I had started my firm. I can't recall the exact location, or even the client, but I certainly remember the student's comments.

We had outlined the crisis scenario for the class and we had tried to anticipate the kinds of questions reporters would ask. It was one of those crisis scenarios that could have been a screenplay for a disaster movie. There were flames, there were injuries, there were deaths. To say it was bad would have been an understatement. This was your worst nightmare! And there were reporters.

I asked the class, seriously mind you, "So what do you tell the reporters?"

One student replied, very seriously, "It's not as bad as they think it is."

The problem was that it was a bad situation. Trying to understate it, masquerade it, or make it seem like a "not-so-bad" situation would have been unbelievable. Yet, that's what the student wanted to say. Why? Because for too many years, that's what corporations had been telling the media in real crisis situations. They like to say it's under control, even when it isn't.

So let's start at the beginning of crisis management.

What is a crisis and how do you know you've got one?

Over the years, I've heard various definitions of crises. I've heard speakers tell me about the Chinese characters that spell out crisis also spell out danger and opportunity. I've read volumes on what a crisis is and I've been lectured on the differences between crises, emergencies, disasters, and issues. I've heard the sound bite. I've read the quotable quote.

My belief after all those years: If it's a real crisis, you'll know it.

A crisis—forget the other definitions—is when something occurs that keeps you from handling your regular business in a normal fashion. It's something that has the *potential*—yes, just the potential—to cause enormous harm to you and/or your organization. It does not have to involve a fire, explosion, or violence in the workplace. No one has to die. No one has to get hurt. It just has to be an issue that has the potential to cause damage in the public arena. It has the potential to damage your corporation's reputation, or your own. A crisis is a turning point or a crossroads where one path leads to control and the other has the potential to lead to disaster.

So, what could go wrong? What could happen? What type of event would cost you your valuable public image? What could ruin your organization's reputation?

> A crisis—forget the other definitions—is when something occurs that keeps you from handling your regular business in a normal fashion. It's something that has the *potential*—yes, just the potential—to cause enormous harm to you and/or your organization.

That's where you start with a crisis plan. That's where you start with crisis management. That's where you start to get a handle on the situation.

Let's start at the beginning.

Whether you're a chemical company, a hospital, a food processor, a high-tech firm, or a manufacturer of automobiles, the first thought generally is: fires and explosions. So start your list there, if it makes sense.

How about product contamination? If it fits, add it to your list.

Strikes? Labor unrest? How about violence in the workplace? Let's say a disgruntled worker—or their spouse—enters the workplace and starts going postal. Hey, we all know too well it can happen.

The next one is more difficult. Let's say the CEO quits, is fired, or dies. You bet that can become a potential crisis.

What about racial discrimination? Sexual harassment? Innovative accounting? Human rights? They've all brought businesses down. Can they bring yours down?

What about environmental issues? Where exactly does that hazardous waste go? What about odors? What about noise? Traffic? Too many lights?

Who makes your raw materials? How are those employees treated? How much are they paid? What about immigrants? It can become international.

What about emissions? What's going out there? How bad is it? Is it a carcinogen? Is it bad? Is it possible? How bad could it be?

What would happen if that tank ruptures? It doesn't really have to happen; it just has to have the potential.

Do some brainstorming. What's your worst nightmare? How bad could it be? What has happened, or could happen, to your competitors? If it can happen to them, could it happen to you?

My longtime friend, associate, and veteran television news anchor, Tom Ryan, likes to tell the story—a true story—that came from one of our early training sessions with a chemical company in Louisiana. We were talking about the possibilities of what could go wrong and this one student—a plant manager—was almost in denial. For him, it was an impossibility. "We have so many safety measures in place," he decried. "An accident of the type you are describing just could not happen." It was unbelievable. It was totally unrealistic.

During the lunch break of our session, the student disappeared momentarily, as many students do. When we resumed the class about 1 P.M., we noticed he was not there. A few minutes later, he stepped in for a few seconds. His face looked the color of someone who had just seen a ghost. His voice was broken. He was nervous. He was scared.

"I'm afraid I won't be able to stay with you," he said. "It seems we've had an emergency at the plant. One of our employees was killed this morning in a freak accident. I really need to get back."

The impossible. The event that couldn't take place had taken place that morning in the middle of our class on crisis management. The unreal suddenly had become all too real. The impossible had happened.

It seems the employee had been using a pole to hasten the release of chemicals from a truck into an auger. The chemicals themselves weren't dangerous. It was the length of the pole and the proximity of the power line.

When the pole connected with the power line, it was all over. The impossible accident had just happened. An employee was dead.

It could just as easily have been a spill of toxic chemicals, a fire, or explosion, but it would not have mattered. The accident was the same, no matter what the cause. The employee was still dead, no matter what the reason.

Never say "never." Over the years, we've been told countless times that the scenarios we present for crisis training are not realistic. Only later do we find out that reality can create far worse nightmares than anything we can brainstorm.

Some of our clients are surprised to find out that many of the so-called crises we get involved in are rather far removed from what you might expect to be a crisis.

There was the art museum that came under fire for exhibiting a collection that offended animal rights activists.

Never say "never." Over the years, we've been told countless times that the scenarios we present for crisis training are not realistic. Only later do we find out that reality can create far worse nightmares than anything we can brainstorm.

Nobody was hurt. Nobody died. But the reaction from the public created a controversy that made the front page of area newspapers, as well as local television stations.

There was the family spat that forced the well-publicized breakup of a large family business.

There was the ever-growing high-tech firm that wanted to move its headquarters to an undeveloped section of the small town it started in. The only problem: local residents didn't want them there. It turned into a major and highly publicized controversy. They ultimately selected another place.

So, even if there's only a slight—ever so slight—possibility that something can happen, include it in your crisis plan. It may not be as remote as you think.

So how do you recognize a crisis? If you think you've got one, you probably do.

DEVELOPING A CRISIS MANAGEMENT STRATEGY

Too often, would-be crisis managers try to develop a solution before they even know the problem. They simply don't do their homework. And most of the time, it shows. If you don't understand the problem, it is going to be difficult to solve it. In order to understand the problem, you need to ask questions. You need to ask a lot of them.

Ask yourself:

- What are the facts? What do we know? What do we need to know? Are we doing everything we can? Have we forgotten anything?

- Have we involved everyone who can help? Are we being objective?

- What about employees? What about customers? What are we telling them? What are they asking? What do they already know?

- What are the public's concerns? What if you were in their shoes? What are they worried about? How could your crisis impact them? What's the perception? What are they saying?

- What, if anything, does the media know? What questions will they ask? What are others telling them? What's being reported?

Once you understand the problem, determine what needs to be done and how to do it.

I received a call from a Midwest-based food company in 1999. They had a problem with food poisoning. Salmonella was detected in one of their products. It had already led to 12 people being hospitalized.

"We just got a call from the health department," the caller said. "I think they're out to get us. I think they want to make an example of us. What should we do?"

"For starters," I told her, "get back on the phone as soon as we hang up and call the health department. Tell them we want to cooperate with them fully. And let them know we're taking every action humanly possible to retrieve every package of food that might be contaminated."

Some people might call this the start of a strategy. I think it was just common sense. We could either work with the health department or fight them. If we fought, we would lose. I'd rather work with them to protect consumers.

So far, the department had not issued a recall. When we took our action, they didn't have to. We were able to take a voluntary action that preempted a mandatory recall. We weren't being *forced* to do anything.

As we got more and more into the crisis, we found the problem occurred because people were not cooking the product properly. The product was "ready to cook," but consumers were interpreting that to mean "ready to eat." They were taking a raw chicken product and throwing it into a microwave for five minutes. It looked okay, but it was still raw inside. They weren't reading the labels and they were paying the consequences.

Despite the voluntary withdrawal of the product, there were still plenty of the chicken products out there and we didn't want more people becoming ill. We always feared the worst, that someone might even die. We needed to get the word out and get it out quickly. We needed help. There was never a question of fighting the media. We needed them.

When developing a crisis management strategy, ask yourself:
• What are the facts?
• Have we involved everyone who can help?
• What about employees?
• What are the public's concerns?
• What, if anything, does the media know?

The health department was receptive to our offer to work with them to solve the problem. They even faxed a copy of their news release to us for review before they issued it. We didn't have to change it. They told it like it was. They said it was a "preparation" problem, but that the company was voluntarily withdrawing the affected product from the marketplace "as a precautionary measure." It was clear we were working with them. We were cooperating.

We offered to exchange or buy back any products that were already out there. Customers were given coupons they could use to buy the company's products. We activated a toll-free hotline to respond to consumer inquires. Hospital expenses were quietly taken care of by company officials. It was never an issue with the company. We just did it.

The salmonella crisis got its share of media attention, but the company was never viewed as the culprit. We were very open with the news media. Coverage was fair. The company had a problem and it was resolving it. I believe people often remember a company more for how they handle a problem than the problem itself. Public opinion this time was the problem was being handled well.

When dealing with the public during a crisis, take the lead early and take control. Get in front and try to see things from the public's perspective.

When the product was reintroduced a few weeks later, it had new packaging with clearly labeled instructions as to how it was to be prepared. There would be no more misinterpretation as to whether it was ready to eat or ready to cook. Whether it was coincidental with all of those coupons the company passed out to its customers or not, today that particular product has a higher market share than before the crisis.

If you reduce crisis management to its simplest form, it is this: Determine what is the right thing to do, and then figure out how to do it. If the crisis becomes known in the public sector, you must decide how to communicate what you've done.

When you're communicating with the public during a crisis, try to follow these simple rules:

> **When communicating with the public during a crisis, follow these simple rules:**
>
> 1. Be absolutely open and honest.
> 2. Less is better.
> 3. Take the lead and take control.
> 4. Speak with one voice.
> 5. Get outside the box.

1. **Be absolutely open and honest.** If it's going to come out anyway, I'd rather be the messenger than someone else, even when the news is bad. I'd rather tell my own story.

2. **Less is better.** Most of the time the less you say, the better off you'll be. If you say too much, your message may be lost in your own clutter. Stay away from too many details. Details just generate more questions and increase the probability that you'll say the wrong thing.

3. **Take the lead and take control.** Don't wait for someone else to get out front. Take the lead early, even if you're not 100 percent ready. You'll never have all the answers. If you wait, you'll just be reacting to someone else's agenda.

4. **Speak with one voice.** It's difficult enough to be consistent with just one spokesperson. Don't make it even tougher. When times do call for more than one spokesperson, make sure they're reading off the same page. Mixed messages are confusing and lead to doubt and distrust and can undermine your credibility.

5. **Get outside the box.** See things the way others see them. Don't operate in a vacuum. Look at the crisis from the outside in. How are others seeing it?

At most of our media training workshops, we walk students through a segment that we generally refer to as message development. For starters, we give them the kind of information they'd have in a real crisis. For the time and date, we try to stick with actual times, so normally the event unfolds about 8:30 or 9 A.M.

We then play a videotape that outlines some key information such as an explosion has taken place, there's a fire, there's a recall, there's an accident in which people have been injured or killed. To the extent possible, we want them to see it happen, not read about it on a piece of paper. We want to make it realistic. We want them to "live it" to the degree possible.

We then move into the kind of information only they can provide. We ask them if the crisis were real, how would they react to it? What actions would they take? What actions would their organization take? The information is written on flipcharts or white boards. As with real life, there's a lot of "facts" we don't know in the beginning. That's okay. That's real.

We then move to questions. What kind of questions

will the media likely ask? What will people want to know? If the tables were turned and you were a local resident impacted by the event, what would you want to know? They have to fight the urge to answer the questions as we develop the list. That will come later, I tell them.

Finally, we move on to the message stage. What is it you want to tell people about the event?

It's not a complex exercise. It generally runs its course in under an hour, often less. But it is a fundamental exercise I use in approaching all kinds of problems, whether it is putting together a message for an interview, developing a business plan, or developing a crisis strategy.

I've had executives tell me they often start their business day with the same kind of exercise. They ask themselves what is going on today? What are the issues? What do we need to do? What's my message today? It's pretty much the same thing.

It's the exercise I run through with my clients as we develop crisis management strategies.

First: What do we know? What are the issues?

Second: What are the concerns? What are the questions? What will people want to know? Remember, you can control your answers, but not the questions. There's almost no end.

Third: What are the actions we need to take? What are the messages we need to convey?

The strategy, of course, will change from crisis to crisis. No two are alike. But the approach to get to the strategy remains pretty much the same.

To assure that I understand the situation correctly, I often write my own analysis of the situation and fire it back to the client. I just want to make sure there are no misunderstandings. It also forces me to make sure I'm not forgetting anything. If you don't understand the situation or you're not aware of a key element, it's difficult to develop a strategy to resolve it.

I often move directly to the "What will they ask?" stage. I begin developing a list of questions that are likely to be asked. It doesn't make any difference whether we have answers or not. It's just important at this point to anticipate the questions.

As the list of questions grows, I then make a stab at trying to answer them. I try to answer them honestly. I try not to put a "spin" on them. To the degree possible, I try to answer them the way the public would want them answered. Some of them don't have answers yet. I leave those blank.

We now have a "situation analysis" that hopefully captures the essence of what happened and what's going on at this moment. We should have a fairly comprehensive list of questions, issues, concerns, and potential answers for some of them.

As we review the responses to the list of questions, the "message" is often staring us right in the face. We just have to be sharp enough to notice it.

The message and ultimately the strategy just make common sense, it often seems. Unfortunately, common-sense messages and commonsense strategies don't come to us automatically. Sometimes we have to work for them.

Your work is just beginning. Now go back once more and try to identify the common themes—the common denominators—in addressing the issues. What are the usable message points or "nuggets"? Are they true? Will they happen? Will people believe them?

Now go back and review the overall list of questions. Can those same common themes and message points address other questions? Ultimately, you should have your two, three, or four key messages. If you have more than that, you're not focused enough. That's the challenge: focus, focus, focus.

You then translate your message into a strategy and begin implementation. In crisis management, it's not enough to simply say the right thing. You have to do it as well.

"Keep it local!" That was the advice from a senior public affairs executive as our hastily assembled crisis team met in a makeshift command center at a Holiday Inn in Northern California.

That particular event involved a deliberately contaminated food product, but it could have been any one of a host of other potential crises.

One question I always try to ask the crisis team and myself when dealing with delicate issues that have strong potential public relations fallout is: Can we keep it local?

Keeping the story local is one way to reduce negative fallout from a crisis. If I'm going to have a bad news situation, I'd rather it be a bad news situation in just one community than the entire country. It's also a lot easier to deal with a problem that is confined to one community than one that has grown legs and become a national issue.

One tactic we try to use in keeping the story local is don't make it seem bigger than it really is by referring reporters to an out-of-town corporate headquarters. If the story is in Des Moines, then the reporter ought to be able to talk to someone in Des Moines.

Keeping the story local is one way to reduce negative fallout from a crisis. If I'm going to have a bad news situation, I'd rather it be a bad news situation in just one community than the entire country.

I don't like to automatically refer reporter calls to some out-of-town public relations executive, or worse yet, to some out-of-town public relations firm. If at all possible, I like to utilize local people who understand the problem and are on top of it. Of course, I also like to utilize local people who have been trained in how to deal with reporters and who have had coaching on what they're likely to be asked and what they might want to say.

Another way to keep a story local is by recognizing the severity of the crisis early and dealing with it head-on at a very early stage. I've often seen potential crises become really big crises just because no one took the action to deal with them when they were still minor crises. Remember, if you don't like airing your dirty laundry in the beginning of a crisis, it will only get worse the longer you wait.

Another way to keep a crisis local is just don't get overly excited. If you remain calm and try to remain in control and on top of the situation, things don't look nearly as bad. Being accessible and responsive to reporters' needs early on also negates some of the potential fallout that can propel a local crisis into the national spotlight. Not talking to the media rarely makes a crisis go away.

Early on in a crisis, there's a time when optimism gets in the way of reality. It's a time when you think there's a better than 50-50 chance that no one will find out. And, if no one knows, why tell them? It's sort of like the tree falling in the forest when there's no one there to hear it. Does it really make a sound? If you have a fire, explosion, product contamination, or a near miss that no one else knows about, did it really happen?

In real life, I'm sure some of the most dramatic crises of our time never made the evening news or the morning newspaper because the news media never knew about them. Some people might say those are the best managed crises of all, at least from a public relations standpoint. But, you have to ask yourself: What if the media would have found out? How would it have played in the media? Would it have come across as "stonewalling" or deceit? Would the organization had been better off to release the information itself anyway?

> Early on in a crisis, there's a time when optimism gets in the way of reality. It's a time when you think there's a better than 50-50 chance that no one will find out.

In most cases, we'll never know. That's why it's often a topic of debate—or at least discussion—in many crisis situations.

You have to determine if you're going to release information on the issue or event, and if so, how and when?

In every crisis situation, no matter whether you ultimately decide to release the information or not, you need to have a strategy for that release. You move forward with preparations for statements, news releases, Q&As, and coached spokespersons regardless. It's hardly a waste of time. It's more like an insurance policy. If you need it, it's there. It certainly beats the alternative.

The ultimate question of whether you "go public," or wait and see if reporters eventually show up at your doorstep is based on numerous factors, including your own corporate philosophy and whether you feel you have a moral responsibility and obligation to publicize even the bad news. Some people argue that it's almost always better to release your own bad news rather than allowing someone else to do it for you. They argue you'll have more control over the information being released. You'll be in the lead, rather than reacting to someone else's agenda.

The reason for that strategy is simple. If the crisis is

bad enough, there's a reasonably good chance that it's going to become public eventually. It's usually just a matter of when.

In the fall of 2001, a metropolitan hospital discovered that one of its nurses had been "misappropriating" a strong painkiller intended for suffering patients.

When a physician prescribed the drug, she would go to the secure cabinet to retrieve it, but the patient never received it. Over a period of months, she had stolen hundreds of vials of the drug. She later confessed she was addicted.

The theft was uncovered by an observant colleague of the nurse who noticed one of the vials had been tampered with. The hospital immediately confronted the nurse, notified police, and pledged cooperation during an investigation.

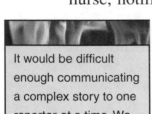

It would be difficult enough communicating a complex story to one reporter at a time. We didn't need a feeding frenzy. That's what can happen with a news briefing if it gets out of hand.

The nurse was placed in a treatment center as the investigation continued. No one knew the whole story, nor how many patients might be affected. No one knew if anyone had been injured, or worse, as a result of the stolen medication.

Early on, there was an argument to go public, even before all the information was known. There was even discussion of conducting a news conference to announce what happened. A Q&A was started. Draft media statements were prepared. We were brought in to coach the hospital spokesperson, the hospital's top executive, who was also a physician.

While we debated how or if we would make the announcement about the nurse, we continued working on communications.

Ultimately, the news conference was canned. It would be difficult enough communicating a complex story to one reporter at a time. We didn't need a feeding frenzy. That's what can happen with a news briefing if it gets out of hand. And in this case, we felt that was a real possibility.

Instead, we decided to talk to each reporter separately. It was a calculated risk, but we felt it would reduce the sensationalism factor and the tendency that occurs sometimes in news briefings when one reporter tries to outdo another.

When the story aired, it was played fairly straightforward. A nurse had done something wrong and she was caught. The hospital was on the side of truth and justice. In no case was the hospital or the nursing staff portrayed as the villain. The nurse had done enough to deserve that title by herself.

The message points:

- What happened was wrong.

- When we first learned of it, we notified authorities immediately.

- We are cooperating fully with authorities.

- Precautions were in place, but no precaution can protect you against someone who violates your trust.

- We will do whatever is necessary to see that this does not happen again.

- And yes, we apologized for anyone who might have suffered as a result of the incident.

Our ace card was the spokesperson. He was a doctor and an administrator, but he was a doctor first. He respected the nurses he worked with, and the last thing he ever wanted to happen was to see someone suffer because of something that went wrong on his watch. He spoke with conviction. He believed what he was saying. He wasn't perfect, but he was believable.

About two months after the very real event played out in the news media, I was working with another hospital in another metropolitan area. It was a new client and we were brought in to provide "refresher" media training for some of their top executives and potential spokespersons. Most of the class was made up of seasoned professionals with plenty of experience in dealing with reporters, even in crisis situations.

For one of the scenarios, I wanted to see how a different hospital with different executives in a different community would deal with the same exact problem we faced earlier that year. I gave them the scenario as it actually happened, only I didn't tell them how the other hospital had reacted to it.

Their initial reaction was surprising.

First of all, most of them didn't think that a nurse stealing drugs intended for patients and forcing patients to suffer needlessly was that big of a deal. Why would you tell the media?

The majority—at least the vocal majority—did not feel the matter needed to be turned over to police. Most did not feel the nurse should have been fired. There seemed to be a consensus that the hospital should "rehabilitate" the nurse quietly and not involve outsiders. At this time, the discussion was being led by administrators.

As the discussion continued, the physicians in the class became more vocal. It wasn't just a nurse using drugs, they said. This was a nurse who was stealing drugs. And she was hurting patients in the process. It was wrong! They felt police should become involved. No one said it, but you could sense they were ashamed of having someone like *that* nurse on their staff.

As the discussion progressed, the doctors seemed to be winning more and more points. They were venting their real feelings. There were three physicians, two nurses, four administrators, and two public relations people in the group. The PR people were maintaining silence. So were the nurses . . . for a while.

Ultimately, the nurses joined up with the doctors. What happened was wrong, they said. The hospital couldn't just stand by and let it go without doing something. They had empathy for the nurse, but they also felt she had done something terribly wrong.

After a lively discussion and the injection of many opinions, the different hospital in the different community with the different people reached the same conclusion as the other hospital. The nurse was immediately suspended and eventually fired. The matter was turned over to authorities. An investigation was launched and anyone possibly affected by the matter was notified.

Then came the matter of what to tell the public. And how?

In the beginning, the push was for a news conference. I suggested it might be difficult, depending on the spokesperson and the media. Normally, I'm not opposed to news briefings, but I felt this one could be an emotionally charged event and one that even a seasoned spokesperson might find difficult.

Finally, they decided to do the same thing the other hospital had done. They issued a media statement and conducted separate interviews.

The message points:

- What happened was wrong.

- Once we discovered what was happening, we immediately took efforts to stop it and notified authorities.

- We are cooperating fully with authorities.

- We're proud of our nursing staff.

- We take every precaution to protect patients from this type of abuse, but ultimately, it becomes a matter of trust. One nurse betrayed that trust.

- And, yes, there was an apology to anyone potentially harmed in any way.

Ultimately, we found that these two very different crisis teams—at two different hospitals in two different cities—had reached the same conclusion on how to deal with the crisis.

That is what crisis teams are all about. They need to collect information, analyze what they know and what they don't know, give thought to the concerns and questions of outsiders, and don't get in a hurry to reach a decision.

They need to fight the urge to determine what needs to be done before they know exactly what happened. They need to fight the urge to develop a solution—and develop an answer—before they know the question.

They need strong leaders, but those leaders need to know that their most important asset may be *listening* to the opinions and thoughts of others. The leaders not only need to listen, but to encourage others to participate. No one should ever go into a crisis strategy meeting with a predetermined idea of what should be done.

- You should always be willing to listen, and if necessary, to change direction.

- Go with the best ideas, no matter where they come from.

- Do the right thing, no matter what it costs.

- Say the right thing, no matter how much it might hurt at the time.

***

It's February 2002. I'm at home, preparing for a flight to Atlanta when my pager goes off. The message: Urgent. RE: Hospital shooting.

I called on my cell phone and then entered my number. I made the call as quickly as possible and then repeated it at least two times before my cell phone rang with the client on the other end of the line.

"It happened last night," the caller said. "The daughter of one of our patients came in to visit her father and then she shot him. He's dead."

Up to this point, police had answered most questions. The hospital had managed to stay in the background. But the rising question in the community was about the safety of the hospital. Was it safe to be a patient (or visitor or employee) at that particular hospital?

Within a matter of a few minutes, the client wanted to know:

- What do we do with the news media?

- What do we tell them?

- Who is our spokesperson?

We agreed to a conference call within 30 minutes. By this time, there were television, radio, and newspaper reporters in the parking lot. The story was already being reported, but there was almost no reaction from the hospital.

I suggested we needed to do a news conference.

"Exactly why is it we're doing a news conference?" asked the CEO.

From my standpoint, I figured there were too many reporters and the story was far too big to do anything else. At this point, my only concern was *who* could do a news conference under these circumstances. Who was our spokesperson?

The answer came quickly. It was the president of the hospital. "Tell me something about the president," I asked. "Well, she's a registered nurse," they said. I was already feeling better. Registered nurses have a unique way of expressing concern and compassion. People believe them.

Within a few minutes, I was talking to our selected spokesperson. She was a natural. She didn't have to worry too much about sound bites. I was concerned about the image she'd leave behind. If people believed her, the words weren't that awfully important.

Within a couple of hours of the call, our registered nurse/hospital president/shooting spokesperson was in front of the news media.

She gave them the simple message. It was one of grief for the family; concern for patients, employees, and visitors; cooperation with authorities; and reassurance that the hospital was safe.

There was another thing about that particular incident.

Approximately one year before, we had conducted a tabletop mock disaster involving a shooting at that hospital. At the time, the possibility seemed remote.

Today, it didn't.

CRISIS PLANS

I t was the first real "crisis plan" I had ever seen. Until then, I'm not sure I had even heard of one. In those days, at least, it wasn't something political reporters came across very often. I'm not sure many others did either.

But now I was a public relations practitioner, having left the field of journalism just a few months earlier. My task was to write a crisis management plan for one of the firm's corporate clients. I had no idea where to start. My boss, a veteran PR professional, provided the document as an example of what a crisis plan should look like. It was interesting.

The "General Instructions" said that the duty of the crisis team member most closely involved in the crisis was to notify the chief of the crisis team. The chief was then to notify other members of the team within "two hours."

The crisis team's responsibilities:

Find out what happened. Answer the questions of who, what, when, where, why, and how—with regard to the problem. Evaluate potential actions that could be taken to solve the problem. Consider long-term as well as short-term implications and recommend appropriate action.

It defined a crisis in rather brief terms:

A crisis is any action that has the potential to adversely affect the company's image with its internal and external public.

The instructions stated that identifying an appropriate spokesperson was essential. The plan warned that, in a crisis, organizations need to speak with one voice. Not a bad idea, I thought, as a former reporter.

Good crisis managers realize that people, not plans, manage crises. No crisis plan has ever had to face TV cameras or answer tough questions from reporters. People do that.

The plan suggested the team develop potential questions and answers that might be used by the spokesperson. In other words, the spokesperson had better be prepared to deal with reporters. The plan further acknowledged the organization's responsibility to talk to the media and the need to call media briefings periodically during the crisis.

Here's the part I think I liked best about it:

The Cardinal Rule for any communication during a crisis or emergency is to TELL IT ALL AND TELL IT FAST.

I kept the plan. It's still in my desk. I still read over its seven pages from time to time. As someone who deals in quotes and sound bites, I admire its brevity and its simplicity.

The crisis plan didn't become caught up in trying to be a textbook instead of a *tool* to aid those facing a crisis. It was pretty much a "seat of your pants" document. It tried to use common sense. The author, I'm sure, had trusted that good managers probably had some sense of what they should do in a crisis. They realized that people, not plans, are the ones who manage crises.

The plan's best advice:

Don't expect to always come out smelling like a rose in a crisis situation.

Sometimes, the best you can do is to avoid stepping in it.

When it comes to crisis plans, I've always felt that companies and organizations needed a document that combined simplicity and comprehension, all tied up in something that would be of real use in a real crisis.

I thought that if a crisis plan was to be worth anything in a real crisis, it ought to be "user friendly." A crisis is not the time to read a textbook; it's a time to deal with the situation at hand. The deeper I delved into crisis management, I found more and more crisis plans that were written to satisfy what the author thought their bosses wanted rather than what they actually needed. Some crisis plans appeared to be written simply to impress people. I'm convinced some authors were being paid by the number of pages they wrote, or the weight of the plan.

There had to be a compromise, somewhere between that simple plan of the 1980s and the more complex documents needed to deal with the problems of the 21st century.

Clients have continually told us they want plans that are easy to read. They want plans that have pre-prepared news releases. They want plans with plenty of checklists. They want to leave nothing to chance. They want the plan to be all inclusive.

In the summer of 1992, I was commissioned to write a crisis plan for a major chemical company. My research— as well as the client's—had determined that most existing plans of the day, including their own, were simply not that good. Most ended up on bookshelves where they would gather dust. They looked good but were rarely used in real crises. They were far from perfect.

So I set out to create what I felt would be the "perfect" crisis plan. It was to be the next generation of crisis plans. It was to be state-of-the-art. It was to be a crisis plan that really worked. It would be comprehensive, yet not cumbersome. It would easily fit in a briefcase. It would not gather dust on a bookshelf.

It would be "user friendly." You wouldn't have to read a manual or take a special class in order to use it. It would be designed to prepare a crisis team before the crisis, yet assume no one would actually read it until a crisis was well under way. It would have a "fail-safe" notification system in which everyone that should be notified in a crisis would be notified. It would be foolproof.

It would anticipate the impossible-to-anticipate crisis. It would have a response for the impossible-to-answer question. It would be soil and water resistant so it could be used when and where it was needed. It would be light. It would be easy to update.

And, I soon began to believe, it would be impossible. I continued my research of existing plans.

One plan I reviewed was so comprehensive that it had to be carried around in a file-folder box. When I looked into the folder marked "First Steps," I found the folder was empty. It was a plan that was sure to make a great impression on someone trying to deal with difficult decisions under near-combat conditions. Another plan was barely a sheet of paper with some phone numbers on it. Most were out of date. Some had innovative ideas, but most were lacking the necessary quality of being easily understood and easy to follow in the middle of a disaster.

I began work on the new plan. After about 75 pages on notification procedures, crisis team responsibilities, setting up crisis centers, and draft media statements and news releases, I went back and started dividing the plan into six logical sections.

INTRODUCTION AND BACKGROUND

This was the part we hoped people would read *before* a crisis, but we were fairly convinced no one would. It included some information on how to use the plan, handling crisis situations and yes, "What constitutes a crisis."

CRISIS TEAM

This section was to offer guidance on how to select a crisis team and provide a description of their specific roles and responsibilities. We didn't think people should serve on a crisis team simply because they had a particular title, but rather because of what they could bring to the team. Too often, we felt, crisis teams were comprised of too many generals and too few soldiers. We didn't want to create an executive committee, but a working team with a strong leader who had both the responsibility and the power to get things done.

Through experience, we knew crisis teams needed more than just people, so we included a section on locating, equipping, and staffing crisis centers and news media centers. The middle of a crisis is not the time to find out you don't have a copy machine, or worse, that no one knows how to run one. We also found that few plans had given much thought as to where reporters would assemble during a crisis. Some had them "herded" into a barren conference room where they were expected to patiently wait for someone to brief them on what was going on. We thought that was a bit optimistic. In real life, it wasn't going to happen. Reporters aren't known for being patient, and they don't like being held prisoner in guarded conference rooms.

> Reporters aren't known for being patient, and they don't like being held prisoner in guarded conference rooms.

We also felt we ought to assign responsibility for maintaining the crisis plan and to keep it up to date. It was a task that shouldn't be left to chance. We also stressed the importance of "post crisis" meetings to find out what worked and what didn't after the crisis was over.

NOTIFICATION PROCEDURES AND INSTRUCTIONS

This section outlined how team members would be contacted, and it contained the list of team members, along with their phone numbers and the names and numbers of other emergency contacts. We hoped team members would read this section before the crisis. The situation would be more difficult if they waited, but the plan would still help guide them, even if they did wait until the last minute.

Now, we came up with the part of the plan we felt would more than likely get used during a real crisis.

FIRST STEPS

Marked with a fire-engine-red tab and referenced throughout the text of the other sections, this was the real heart of the plan. This part told them what they needed to do and how to do it even if they had never read the plan before. It would tell them where to find whatever they needed. It was a major cross-reference to everything else in the plan. It was simple, though, and easy to use. In many ways, this *was* the plan.

NEWS MEDIA

This section was a major resource in the plan. If you've ever tried to draft a media statement in the heat of a crisis, you would appreciate this section more than anything. We had tried to anticipate the various kinds of crises that could impact the company, and we had drafted media statements and news releases to deal with them. It was better than a "fill-in-the-blanks" news media statement, because we had already ran these past senior management and the legal staff. We even took a stab at potential media questions and suggested responses. The section even walked them through staging a news conference, should it become necessary.

GENERAL INFORMATION AND CONTACTS

This section contained all types of information on plant sites, contacts, directions on how to get there, nearby hotels, local public officials, brief histories, and background information on what the plant produced. It was the kind of information we felt people would need in a crisis and we wanted to make it easy to find. There were even contact numbers on chartering aircraft, if necessary.

The final plan was approximately 100 pages long, but the First Steps section, the real meat of the plan, was scaled down to under 20 pages. This crucial section was designed to walk someone through what needed to be done on its own. It was designed to be a part of the plan or a simple stand-alone document.

After we decided we had most of the bases covered, we selected an easy-to-read type style, easy-to-understand headlines, flowcharts, and fill-in-the-blanks lists of every kind, and then we printed it on a water-resistant paper with a colored index page and matching sub-index pages with tabs for each subsection.

Finally, we borrowed an "about this plan" message from one of our earlier documents—signed by the client's CEO—to give our plan his personal corporate blessing. We were impressed with ourselves.

Then we started testing it.

We put together an ad hoc crisis team and created some scenarios for it to see how well the plan would work under field conditions. By design, the team that would test the plan had never before seen the document. We thought that would be the only realistic test. We were pleasantly surprised. It worked. And we were convinced it might have worked even better had they read it before the test.

That plan was barely completed when we decided it was already outdated and time for the next generation. We wanted a computerized crisis plan.

I've been involved with computers since my early days as a political reporter. The news media was one of the first industries to discover how computerization could save time and money. I began asking seasoned computer programmers about the possibility of a computerized crisis plan. There was a lot of interest.

Unfortunately, I found that the computer people I talked to didn't understand crisis management and I certainly knew little to nothing about computer programming.

Not until the Internet exploded did we begin to see how crisis plans and computers could work together. The Internet is full of Web sites that allow you to move freely from one Web page to another with the click of a mouse. If you don't know where to find something, you just use a search engine. The information is all there and it's relatively easy to find. Could the same approach be directed toward a crisis plan? I wasn't sure.

My son, Jeff, was now working with our organization, and he was intrigued with the possibilities of the Internet and Web sites. He's a self-taught computer whiz. He speaks a completely different language than most of us, but he totally understands computers.

He had our firm on the World Wide Web when I was still trying to figure out what the Web was. He created and still maintains our firm's Web site, as well as Web sites for several of our clients. He was also familiar with the crisis plans we had written since he had been instrumental in their design and formatting.

So it wasn't that surprising that I turned to Jeff to design our first computerized crisis plan. The end result was a plan that could be complex, but easy to use. If you didn't know what to look for, just type in a word on the plan's search engine. It worked.

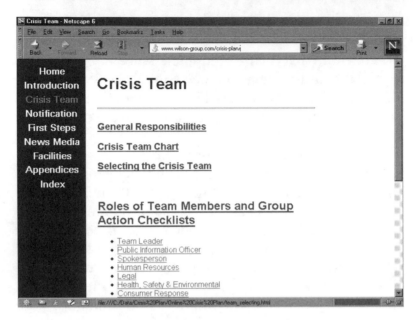

Computerized crisis plans are formatted in such a way that they can be comprehensive, yet still easy to use.

Unlike the bulky documents in three-ring binders, the new plan could be carried on a laptop computer or accessed over a corporate intranet or over the Internet—with proper security.

It carried the simplicity of that first document: "Tell it all and tell it fast," along with the comprehensiveness of the later documents with all their standard news releases, phone lists, directions, and checklists.

The electronic version allowed us to create more comprehensive plans and allowed plans to be updated instantly. We're already on our third generation of computerized plans, and I'm convinced there's no end in sight.

As with any plan, my only concern is that team members might become overly dependent on it. And, as good as the plans are today, they're still only a resource. It still takes people to manage a crisis.

In our media training sessions, I often warn students: If you don't want to be quoted on something, don't say it. The same thing goes with crisis plans and any kind of document that might be connected to a crisis. If you don't want to see it on the front page of the *New York Times*, don't put it on paper in the first place.

One of the tests I put crisis plans through is this: What would happen if the crisis plan itself became public and the news media decided to run all of it or portions of it in a newspaper or magazine? If you can't live with the idea of seeing your prized crisis plan in your local newspaper, then you probably don't have such a good plan after all. What is it that you placed in the document that would be embarrassing if a reporter got a copy of it? How much embarrassment can you and your organization stand?

> If you can't live with the idea of seeing your prized crisis plan in your local newspaper, then you probably don't have such a good plan after all.

As a former reporter, I was concerned from the beginning with some of the material that was contained in crisis plans and the multitude of other documents that might be related to the handling of a specific crisis or issue.

By its very nature, some of the information contained in crisis plans is an eye opener of what could possibly happen to your organization and how you would deal with it. The fact that your plan deals with fires, explosions, chemical spills, and employee violence might be interpreted to mean that you expect such events.

And don't say it can't happen. It can and it has. I know of at least one large corporation that had egg on its face when its internal crisis plan became public. Undoubtedly, there are others. Some corporate crisis plans are available through professional associations. Some have even been entered into competition for awards. I've been very proud of some of the plans I've authored over the years, but they're written for clients, not the news media. They're confidential documents that I try to keep protected.

We protect our computerized plans, and the client normally increases security significantly.

Hard copy plans are normally numbered. They go only to team members who sign for them. We ask that they keep them confidential. Old plans, when turned in, are normally shredded.

There's usually an "invisible" section of our plans that deals with "What happens if the plan becomes public?" That section is verbally transmitted to team members who should be fully aware of the consequences.

I started that section when we were involved in a major plant closing. We knew at least three months ahead of time that we'd probably have to close down the plant. It was one of several plants the company was acquiring as part of the acquisition of another company. Our client wanted to buy the other company, but it had no real use for the plant. When I was brought in, the decision to close the plant hadn't been made yet, although it was starting to look pretty certain.

A lot of things needed to be done if we closed the plant, and accomplishing them would be difficult once word got out that the plant was closing.

We began to put together a plan that dealt specifically with the possible plant closing. It covered all bases, including the possibility that the plant would remain open. But the plan dealt heavily with the growing probability that the plant would close. We put together a timeline, contact lists, probable news releases, and a Q&A that left almost nothing to chance. It also included what we would do if word got out prematurely that the plant would close, or if—heaven forbid—that the plan itself was leaked to the media.

While this might all sound like a cruel joke to those people who worked at the plant, you have to realize that no decision had been made yet on whether the plant would be closed and that until the acquisition was complete, no decision could be made.

The one thing everyone insisted on was that if we did close the plant, we would do it with dignity. Employees would be treated with respect, and we would do everything we could to help them find other employment. We were also committed to working with the community to find a new occupant for the plant, and we were prepared to back that commitment with money.

The announcement would be made as soon as a decision was made. Key plant officials and key officials in the community would be told of the action at approximately the same time. Managers and supervisors would then be told and then the remaining workers would—to the degree possible—be told all at the same time as one group. Once employees were told, the media would be advised. We simply didn't feel it was right to tell reporters, until those most impacted by the event knew it themselves.

Had rumors of the closing leaked out prematurely, we were prepared to say honestly that a closing was under consideration, but that no decision had been made yet.

When the plant was closed, it was a pretty big news story. Not all of it was good. Some of it was critical. But for the most part, it was fair.

FIRST STEPS

It was Saturday morning and I was sitting at the kitchen table having my second or third cup of coffee and reading the newspaper when my alphanumeric pager began buzzing. My first thought was that it was probably just another case of someone calling the wrong number. Northwest Airlines, I had discovered, had a toll-free number that wasn't that far from our 800 number. Over the years, we had returned several calls we thought were possible clients only to find out it was a disgruntled passenger trying to find his lost bags in Detroit. I guess that too can be a crisis, but not the kind I can help with a lot. I'm still trying to find the bags U.S. Airways lost last spring.

So, who would be calling my office on a Saturday morning? I looked. The telephone number was not familiar. Neither was the name. Even the message was unclear. My first thought was that someone was trying to sell me a credit card. What the heck, I thought. It can't hurt to find out what they want.

I called the number, not expecting much more than another person complaining that Northwest had lost their luggage.

There was a lawyer on the other end of the line. He sounded a bit nervous, but he had a pleasant voice. I felt better.

"Sorry to bother you on a Saturday morning," he said. "But we have a problem here and I was asked to call you. I've been told you specialize in situations like this."

"What kind of situation do you have?" I asked.

"It's kind of complicated," he continued. "But let's just say it involves a pretty large gasoline spill. We've been getting a lot of media attention. How soon can you be here?"

I found out that "here" wasn't all that far away. I thought if I left right away, I could be there by mid-afternoon.

As I drove to the scene of the spill, there were numerous fire trucks and emergency vehicles. Off in the distance, I could see two or more large petroleum storage tanks. What looked like a white house trailer was parked on the side of the hill with several oil company trucks parked around it. It looked like the command center. The fact that it said "Emergency Operations Center" on the side was a good clue. I pointed my car toward the trailer.

When I got out of the car, a man walked toward me and introduced himself as Patrick. He was the one who called me. One of his bosses whom I had worked with in the past at the oil company had suggested he contact me.

I arrived just in time for the latest briefing from the incident commander.

He said a large storage tank along an underground pipeline had been taken out of commission for normal repairs. All of the gasoline had been pumped out of the tank for the procedure, and once completed it was to be refilled. That's what was supposedly happening earlier in the week. The only problem was that there was a break in the pipeline just outside of the tank. The break was underground and went undetected. As they attempted to pump gasoline back into the tank, it never made it there. For hours and hours, the high-test gasoline was pumped directly into the ground.

It was a suburban neighborhood and several residents smelled what they thought was gasoline inside their basements. The fire department was called. Homes were evacuated and the oil company was contacted.

When they had first arrived shortly after the spill, the oil company's emergency response team assessed the situation and began actions to stop the spread of the leaking gasoline. It was during part of that cleanup operation that a backhoe apparently struck a rock. It caused a spark. The gasoline vapors ignited.

Three firefighters were slightly injured. The smoke and flames—coupled with injured firemen—were part of a "made-for-TV" news story.

The company's public affairs officer was handling the media pretty well, but there was concern that more needed to be done. I thought we needed more of a "corporate face" on the story. I began coaching a senior official with the company to talk to reporters. It would be a new experience for him, but he adapted quickly. He was a natural. He came across as authoritative, concerned, compassionate, and sincere. I couldn't ask for much more.

It wasn't enough, however, to have a senior executive saying the right thing. We had to do the right thing as well.

Attention turned to the dislocated residents. Where would they go?

We found a local hotel that could accommodate them and arranged for everything they needed. No one ever asked what it would cost. It didn't matter. It had to be done.

Later, at a public meeting where I served as the facilitator between local residents and the oil company, most residents clearly felt the company had done what it could. It was a bad situation, but they were making the most of it.

Of course some people were upset and nothing would make them feel better, but they were a minority.

Families were genuinely concerned with health effects caused by the spill. What would it do to their children? We had anticipated the question and had arranged for a respected and well-spoken toxicologist to address that concern. It was something a company executive just couldn't do with any degree of credibility.

We had experts to address just about any potential concern, and we had state and local officials there. The chief of police and the fire chief had been contacted and were there with us. They had credibility in the community. At best, we were outsiders. We knew we had a message we needed to get across. We also knew we were there to listen. That particular night, listening was more important than talking.

Several television stations and newspapers had sent reporters to cover the meeting. They talked to local residents and they talked to us. The message was pretty much the same. It had been a terrible accident, but the oil company was committed to doing whatever was necessary to make it right.

> Sometimes, the most difficult task is to determine exactly what "the right thing" is. When in doubt, I try to place myself in the shoes of those most closely impacted and ask, "What would I want them to do? What would I expect?"

We knew we had to do "the right thing" no matter how long it took, no matter how difficult and no matter the cost.

I look back now at that event from time to time and remind myself that in a crisis, companies and organizations really have no choice but to do "the right thing." Ultimately, they're going to have to do it anyway. No one should have to force them to do it. The right thing should be done voluntarily and it should be done quickly.

Sometimes, the most difficult task is to determine exactly what "the right thing" is. When in doubt, I try to place myself in the shoes of those most closely impacted and ask, "What would I want them to do? What would I expect?"

Answer those questions honestly and you'll probably soon determine what needs to be done. The next step is to do the right thing and then communicate what you've done.

Often, by the time a client or would-be client calls my office, they're already well into the midst of a crisis. The initial steps—right or wrong—have already been taken. They know they're in trouble and they're grasping at anything and anyone who might help remedy a bad situation. They know what they've done, they're just not sure what they need to do next. Often, they're afraid to do anything more, lest it make the situation worse.

It's probably human nature to hope that bad things will just go away, that nobody will notice. Unfortunately, it's not good crisis management.

> It's probably human nature to hope that bad things will just go away, that nobody will notice. Unfortunately, it's not good crisis management.

Once you recognize you have a crisis—or the potential for one—you need to start taking key steps. In crisis management, those first steps are among the most important steps you'll ever take.

Step Number One

Gather as much information about the situation as you can.

When I lecture on crisis management, I tell people that early on in a crisis, you need to keep two separate charts. On one chart, you begin listing what you know about the crisis. What happened? Who is involved? Where did it take place? Is the public involved or at risk? What's going on right now? You want to answer the boilerplate questions such as Who, What, When, Where, How, and Why, and then move on from there. Chances are you'll have some gaps.

On the other chart, you want to begin listing those things and/or information that you don't know: things like the suspected cause, potential impact externally and internally, short-term and long-term prognosis, and potential outcome. In other words: What caused it? Could it get worse? In the beginning, it's normally a much longer list.

When the list of what you know begins to outnumber what you don't know, only then can you start getting a real grasp of the situation.

Seven Key Steps to Take When You Recognize a Real or Potential Crisis

1. Gather as much information about the situation as you can.

2. Alert key members of your crisis team.

3. Assign tasks and continue fact-finding.

4. Develop potential solutions.

5. Implement your solution.

6. Communicate what you are doing.

7. Review the actions, messages, and ultimate outcome.

Step Number Two

About the same time that you realize you have a potential crisis, you need to start alerting key members of your crisis team. They ought to be able to help you complete Step Number One. Tell them what you know. Use them as a sounding board.

The keys to Step Number Two are (1) knowing who to notify and (2) knowing how they can be notified.

The people who need to be notified will change depending on the crisis. In some situations, you may need the services of a health and safety specialist much more than your chief financial officer. In others, the chief financial officer may be integral to the crisis.

Regardless of the nature of your crisis, you should have a core team of members you call every time. It may be just three, four, or five individuals. Their titles will vary, but they ultimately become the heart of your crisis team.

STEP NUMBER THREE

Assign tasks and continue fact-finding. Simply put, you can't manage a crisis if you don't know what the crisis is. Make sure you examine the crisis from all angles. One person can't do that. The tasks need to be delegated. Throughout the process, don't be afraid to keep asking questions.

STEP NUMBER FOUR

Develop potential solutions. You can't manage a crisis without a solution. What are the various potential scenarios? Think them out. Which ones are even practical? Which one is best? What can be done now? Listen, listen, listen. You never know where the best solution will come from. Don't discount even the most wild ideas too soon. They might just work.

STEP NUMBER FIVE

Implement your solution. This is the hard part. Now you actually have to do what you said you could do. It takes people, resources, money, and time. Make sure you have all the pieces to make it work. Hopefully, you haven't bitten off more than you can chew.

STEP NUMBER SIX

Communicate what you are doing. If this is a public crisis playing out in the news media, you need to tell people what you're doing and why. This step should not be treated lightly. It may not be enough to do the right thing if no one knows you did it. If there is a communications vacuum, it may be filled with fear and rumors, but rest assured, it will be filled. Don't wait for someone else to tell your story. Take the lead!

STEP NUMBER SEVEN

Review the actions, messages, and ultimate outcome. What went right? What went wrong? How could you do it better? What follow-up actions will be necessary? If the crisis plan needs to be adjusted, now is the time to adjust it. If the makeup of the crisis team needs to be changed, now is a good time to change it.

How you respond to the news media during those first few minutes of a crisis can be just as important in the public's eye as how you handle the crisis itself.

I've compared it to what trauma physicians refer to as "that golden hour of opportunity." In a trauma case, I'm told there may be up to an hour where the right action can make the difference between life and death. It's how fast you can react and obtain critical medical care.

In a crisis, the window of opportunity for dealing with the news media isn't much longer.

Your first impression is often a lasting impression. What people see and hear about the crisis during those first few moments could influence their opinion of how you handled the crisis. If you say nothing at all, you're leaving that impression for others to make for you.

There was an industrial explosion near Dayton, Ohio, a few years ago that attracted a great deal of television coverage. Helicopters were flying over the smoke-filled scene. You could see the flashing red lights of fire trucks and ambulances below.

The reporters were reporting the story, but at this point, there were no company officials to tell them what was going on. One reporter found an employee, a union member with a degree of seniority at the plant.

He began his report: "What is that area of the plant like where the explosion took place? I talked with a union member at the plant, and he told us what that area was like."

"They got gas, they got blast furnace gas, they got everything there for an explosion," he told the reporter with a bit of a grin on his face. "And our job is to see that we don't have an explosion. It's scary. It's nerve-racking. I've been here 23 years and I've seen seven people get killed.

"So, you know, it ain't like working at K-Mart," he finished.

"And I'm sure that comment would be ratified by just about everybody who works here," the reporter added.

It may not have been what the company wanted to say, but it sure was a sound bite. That comment became the story. Had the company had someone there to talk to the reporter, things might have worked out differently. Sure, the reporter still might have found a quotable employee, but hopefully his comments would have been balanced by the spokesperson's message.

In this case, the company created a vacuum and someone else filled it.

Just because you're not ready to talk to the news media

> Just because you're not ready to talk to the news media will never stop or slow down news coverage. The story will continue with you—or without you. If you create a vacuum by your absence, it will be filled by someone else.

will never stop or slow down news coverage. The story will continue with you—or without you. If you create a vacuum by your absence, it will be filled by someone else.

In a crisis, reporters don't want, nor will they wait for, a "prepared media statement" or a staged news conference. They want to know what happened and they want to know it now.

That's why it's important to have on-site spokespersons who can deal with reporters during those crucial first moments, even when they don't have all the answers. In a crisis, take the lead and present an up-front and honest media response. Good frontline spokespersons need to be as accurate as possible. If they are not sure about something, they don't say it. They never speculate. They are not afraid to tell reporters what they know, as well as what they don't know.

Remember, if you're not talking to the news media during a crisis, someone else will. And rest assured, others are probably not interested in your message.

I remember a chemical plant explosion a few years ago when more than two hours passed before the plant manager was available to talk to the throng of reporters covering the event. By that time, they had already interviewed his employees, local residents, firefighters, and disgruntled former employees on live television. They had interviewed just about everyone except for the plant spokesperson, who was not available.

So what can you tell reporters in a crisis when there is little information to report?

Start with the obvious. If a building is in flames, it is fairly safe to say you have a fire. In most instances, it is fairly safe to say your organization and/or local firefighters are doing whatever they can to bring it under control. And it should be safe to say that your primary concern is the safety of your workers and the community.

Reporters know you won't have answers for all of their questions. Answers to other questions can probably wait.

As a reporter friend of mine says, "We don't expect everything right away. Just give us what you can."

Another reporter I know says we could all learn a lesson from those lion tamers at the circus. She says one of the reasons those ferocious lions don't attack the trainer is that he keeps throwing them a bone from time to time. She says the same goes for reporters. Don't be afraid to throw them a bone now and then.

Remember that not being available during those initial moments can be interpreted as "no comment," that you're hiding something, or you simply don't care. Saying almost anything is usually better than saying nothing.

Project an image early that you are concerned and that you are in control. Reassure people that your organization knows what it's doing and it is doing the right thing.

DEALING WITH THE NEWS MEDIA

Many of the students who enter our media training workshops have an absolute fear of being interviewed by a reporter. In survey after survey, they tell us their biggest fear is that they'll say something that will make them look stupid, or worse: make their company look bad.

They say they're afraid they'll be misquoted, or quoted out of context. They're afraid reporters will manipulate the story to meet their own agenda. Many have a strong distrust of the news media. They've all heard horror stories about others who have suffered bad experiences in media interviews, and they're afraid the same thing will happen to them.

Many are convinced that all—or at least most—reporters are out to get them, that reporters have a predetermined agenda and they'll never let the facts get in the way of a good story.

Some of that fear is founded in fact. Unfortunately, some of it is inspired by the very people their companies pay to prepare them to handle media interviews. Many of the horror stories I hear about reporters didn't take place at a newspaper or television station, but in a media training class. In other words, it was a make-believe situation. It never really happened.

One student tells the story of how he was blindfolded and led into a dark room where he was ordered to sit down on a chair. Suddenly a television light is shining in his face and a hostile reporter is asking him angry questions. It sounds more like an interrogation than a media interview. It's also not reality.

Although some clients want us to provide the "in-your-face" interview with interrogating questions, it's not the real world. If you're training someone to deal with the news media, I would think the concept would be to increase their comfort level and self-confidence. I'm not sure that scaring someone does that at all.

Almost everyone is at least a little nervous about facing the news media in times of crisis, but most interviews are not hostile.

The vast majority of all media interviews are not hostile. They are not interrogations. They are between reporters who want and need information to do their stories and the people they hope can provide that information.

When we first started conducting media training classes, I fell into the trap of doing them in an "interrogation style," partially because that's what a lot of companies were telling us they wanted in those days. It was what they were used to. It is what they thought reporters were like.

I recall at the end of one of those early classes, we were asking people what they had learned during the session. We wanted to know their impressions. We wanted to know if they liked it.

One of the students told us something I will always remember, and his comments forever changed the way we conduct media training classes.

"The one thing I learned today was to never talk to a reporter," he said.

It was the last thing we wanted to accomplish. We were trying to prepare people to deal with the news media, not to scare them away.

A few years ago, I was working with an oil company executive whose company felt he needed to improve his media skills. It was certainly not an uncommon request. In today's world, media and/or communications skills are an important part of business, at least for successful business executives.

We were conducting the training in his office suite. The interview was to be based on real-life situations facing his organization. It wasn't that different from the kind of interviews I had done in my previous life as a reporter.

We were both seated. The television camera was mounted on a tripod behind me. We both had lavalier microphones fastened to our ties. We were using only modest lights. It didn't seem all that threatening at the time.

I had just begun my line of questioning. The questions weren't tough. They were not terribly intimidating, I thought. It was just another interview. I wanted to learn more about his company and where it was headed.

The first thing I noticed was the fidgeting. He couldn't sit still. His hands were visibly shaking. His lips began quivering a bit and then the sweat broke out on his face. He certainly was not comfortable with what we were doing. I was more than a little worried.

I knew we had a problem. I asked my cameraman to shut off the camera and lights and suggested we take a break, even though we had barely started.

"What's the problem?" I asked. "You just seem a little nervous."

"This isn't the first time I've gone through this kind of training," he said. "I went through it a few years ago with another firm."

There was a long pause, followed by a deep breath and then:

"It was the worst experience of my life."

I didn't ask for the details, but let it suffice that the only thing his prior training had accomplished was to scare him from ever wanting to deal with a reporter. And even though he had risen to a very high position within his company, he had managed to avoid being interviewed except under the most favorable circumstances. That wouldn't be the case if he stepped into the CEO's suite down the hall. In today's world, it's difficult to avoid interviews when you're the head of the company.

I told him I was sorry his last experience had not worked out that well, and I told him that most interviews are relatively painless. Most of the fear, I told him, is created by our own anxiety in doing the interview, not by the reporter. It's sort of like giving a speech. The fear of doing the speech is usually much worse than giving the speech itself. Once you get past the camera, microphone, and lights, it's just an on-the-record conversation.

We continued the training. He relaxed a bit, but it was clear he'd never be able to completely shake the fear of that prior training. It's a shame. He probably would have made a good spokesperson for his company. He believed in his company. He was honest. He knew what to say. He was just afraid of reporters. Whatever had happened to him in his previous training would stay with him the rest of his life.

He retired a few years later. It was a bit early. He never made it into the CEO's office.

Being interviewed by a reporter is not a comfortable experience. I've been on both sides of interviews, and I can tell you I'd rather be the person asking the questions than the person answering them.

But an interview is not an interrogation. At least it shouldn't be. An interview is a way a reporter gathers information for a story. Sure, some reporters try to use theatrics rather than journalistic skills, but those kinds of reporters are rare.

For most of us—the vast majority of us—media interviews are not going to resemble a *60 Minutes* interview. Even *60 Minutes* interviews don't resemble what many people think they are. For most of us, the reporter is not trying to get us; he or she is simply trying to get a story.

> But an interview is not an interrogation. At least it shouldn't be. An interview is a way a reporter gathers information for a story. Sure, some reporters try to use theatrics rather than journalistic skills, but those kinds of reporters are rare.

The majority of those people who go through our media training classes have been interviewed very few times, if at all. Most have little experience in dealing with the news media. They dwell more on the possibility of failure than success. It's amazing to watch their faces when they do see themselves on videotape. For most of them, the videotape is much better than they imagined. "Hey, I'm not that bad," I've heard some of them say.

Our intent in media training is to raise the confidence level of those people in our class. We want them to be comfortable in their ability to communicate their message. We want them to concentrate on their message and what they want to communicate, rather than the next question the reporter will ask, which is a big problem in interviews. Often, the person being interviewed is so concerned about what will happen next—the next question—that they don't pay enough attention to the question they're addressing now. That's dangerous.

If you're thinking of one thing and talking about another, who knows what you'll say?

That's why so many of us get misquoted. It's not that we really are misquoted; it's just that we weren't thinking while we were talking. One of my students described it best. He said it's like your mouth is going 90 miles per hour, but your brain is stuck on 30.

So how do you combat what is so much human nature?

I begin every media training workshop with this warning: "Never do an interview just to answer the reporter's question."

Now, some reporters—and others—might find exception with that. I'm not saying there's anything wrong with answering the reporter's question; I'm just saying that answering the question is simply not enough.

In most cases, there's nothing wrong with answering a reporter's question, even when the answer is "I don't know." What I'm saying is that "I don't know" is not enough. You should have a message you want to communicate. If you don't, you probably shouldn't be doing the interview in the first place.

Second: I tell students that you should never assume the reporter knows what you are talking about.

There's a perception—or misperception—in corporate America that reporters are specialists. For the most part, they are not. The reporter covering the story where five of your employees were shot by one of their colleagues is not a specialist on the subject; he or she was simply available at the time to cover the story. The same goes with fires and explosions.

I was a political reporter for most of my career in journalism, yet I still covered my fair share of shootings, explosions, and whatever else happened when I wasn't busy doing something else. When I was a news bureau chief in Chicago, I covered all types of stories from product tamperings to oil spills to stories on offbeat religions. Why? Because I was in the area and I was available. I remember covering a large number of health-care stories. It wasn't because I was a health-care reporter. It was because Chicago was the home of the American Medical Association and therefore generated a large number of health-care stories.

> I've often said that reporters know only three types of chemicals. There are toxic chemicals, deadly chemicals, and chemicals that cause cancer.

The reporter assigned to cover a crisis may be assigned because of his or her availability and proximity to where the event takes place. It may have nothing to do with their expertise in whatever you do.

As a result, you may have to "educate" the reporter not only on the event, but about your industry and what you do.

I've often said that reporters know only three types of chemicals. There are toxic chemicals, deadly chemicals,

and chemicals that cause cancer. They simply repeat public opinion. It's not that they're stupid. They are not. It's
not that they are not educated; they are. The problem is
that reporters are generalists. They know a lot about a lot
of things. If they were that good at chemistry, they might
have chosen another career, but that's another story.

As a result, we not only have to inform, but we also
have to teach. If done correctly, reporters don't mind. If
they weren't inquisitive in the first place, they would
have never become reporters. They like learning. They
like learning a lot about a lot of things.

Reporters have to do the story with the information
they have. If you don't explain things in a way the aver-
age person can understand, the reporter will have to do
it for you. Too often, the reporter can't use what you say
because it is not quotable, or because the general public
just wouldn't understand it. Too often, reporters are
forced to translate what they "think" someone was saying, rather than what you actually said because what
you said wasn't comprehensible to the reporter or the
general public.

If you don't tell them what something means, someone else will. That might not be in your best interest.
Given a choice in a crisis, I'd much rather have a reporter who knows what he's talking about.

So what do you tell reporters in a crisis?

I'm sure some people would say "as little as possible."
I don't agree, although I do think you can say too much.

I think you tell them what you can. In most crises,
there's nothing wrong with telling reporters "what happened" to the extent that you know what happened. You
can usually tell them what you're doing about it. You can
probably tell them when it happened and where it happened. But that's not enough. You have to have a message.
You don't want to simply answer reporters' questions.

In our media training classes, I tell students the entire class can be broken into three parts. *First*: Know your message!

So what is your message? What is it you want to tell reporters? What is it you want to tell the public? Your message will change from time to time. What you tell reporters in a chemical spill may be a lot different than what you would tell them when the CEO's plane goes down in Ecuador.

But I believe we can use some areas as common denominators in almost any crisis. At least this should prompt you to come up with the right message. In almost any crisis, the public wants to know what happened. What caused it? What are you doing about it? So, tell the media what you can tell them. Give them the facts. But giving them the facts doesn't mean giving them everything you know. Give them what they need to tell their story. And make sure what you give them is absolutely accurate. In crisis management, there's no excuse—whatsoever—for giving out false information.

> **Three Parts of Deaing with the Media:**
>
> 1. Know your message!
>
> 2. Package your message!
>
> 3. Deliver your message with conviction!

Try to answer the questions to what, or what happened? When? Where? Why? How? In many cases, you won't have answers to every question, at least not in the beginning. That's okay. Reporters may want answers to all of their questions, but good reporters know not all questions have answers.

People want to be reassured in a crisis that you're in CONTROL of the situation. So, it's important to let them know—if we can—that we are in control. But remember that what you say has to sound credible. So saying "We're in control of the situation" probably won't work if you're standing in front of a burning building. It not only has to be true. It has to be believable.

In a crisis, I've sometimes said, there are only three kinds of situations: situations that are under control, situations that are being brought under control, and situations where we are doing everything we can to bring them under control. It's not real reassuring to the public to hear that things "are out of control." We want to reassure the public that we're on top of the situation, that we know what we're doing. So how do you do that?

Telling the public what you're doing about the crisis can carry the message that the situation is under control, or at least you are in control of the situation.

If it is true, you can say that you have trained emergency personnel responding to the situation. Hopefully, that is the case. If it is true, you can say the fire/explosion, etc., is "isolated" or "contained." It's not the same as saying the situation is under control, but it's close.

You also can tell them what you are doing about the situation. You can tell them that firefighters are on the scene and are doing everything they can at this time to bring the situation under control.

I'm convinced the public understands that bad things happen. They understand that people even make mistakes. What they want to hear in a crisis is what you're doing about it. They want to know how it affects them.

Your next message is CONCERN. What is your major concern?

It depends on the nature of the crisis, but often, if you answer that question honestly, it is the safety of those affected: your workers and the people in the community. If you are not concerned about people, you're not very human. In our workshops, I advise students to simply finish this sentence if they ever are at a loss for words in an interview: "Right now, our *primary* concern is. . . ."

If anyone is injured, killed, or missing, demonstrating

COMPASSION is important. We don't advise people to say, "We have compassion." We tell them to show it. In a real crisis, it's not that difficult.

What about COOPERATION? In a crisis, you may find yourself depending upon firefighters, police officers, and even the public to assist. If that's the case, it may be part of your message.

"Right now, we are cooperating fully with law enforcement officials. . . ."

"I want to thank local residents for their cooperation."

Finally, there is PRAISE. In many of the crises I've been involved in, employees have taken that extra step to help. Firefighters have risked their lives to protect others. Are you proud of the way your employees reacted? Did firefighters do a good job? If they did, say it!

"Local firefighters and law enforcement officials did a fantastic job."

"I am extremely proud of the way our employees responded to this tragic situation."

I was asked recently if someone other than the general manager, the site manager, or the president could say that. I thought briefly, and my answer was yes. You don't have to be the top executive to be proud of your employees or your colleagues.

This isn't spin control. It's simply giving credit where credit is due. If someone does a great job, let the world know it.

Okay, so now you know your message. What do you do with it? You have to package it so the news media can use it.

If you want the news media to use your message, it must be packaged in a nugget, quotable quote, or sound bite.

If you watch television or read newspapers, you'll never get a complete picture of what happened. That's because reporters and editors can only take pieces of interviews and put them on television or in the newspaper. What they choose to use is called a "sound bite" or sometimes a "quotable quote." Few newscasts or newspapers have the luxury of providing readers, listeners, or viewers with everything that was said. It's like seeing a few frames of a film rather than the entire movie.

I like to refer to them as nuggets. It's the part of the interview that actually gets used. It's what the reporter chooses to use to tell their story.

So, if you want to get quoted, you have to be quotable.

So, how do you speak in nuggets?

First, nuggets cannot be read. No one takes a spokesperson seriously if he or she has to read their sound bites.

Second, nuggets cannot be canned. Reporters don't like canned statements. They like real quotes from real people.

Real nuggets come from the heart, not the head. They are impromptu. They are real. I continually tell students that if you know what you're talking about and you know your message, the sound bites will take care of themselves. And they do.

Finally, I tell students that it's not enough to know your message and package it in sound bites. You have to be believable. Credibility is essential in a crisis situation. If people don't believe you, it doesn't make any difference what you say.

In order to be believable, you first have to believe it yourself.

Everything you say to a reporter has to pass the test of ownership. Are you comfortable saying it? Can you say it in your own words? Can you say it in your own style? Do you believe it?

> If you know what you're talking about and you know your message, the sound bites will take care of themselves.

As singer and songwriter Willie Nelson has been quoted as saying, "If you don't believe the lyrics, you can't sing the song. Ain't nobody that good of a liar."

If you've ever watched the Sunday morning news/talk shows, there's no doubt you've watched and listened as some politician looked a reporter right in the eyes—totally ignored his question—and then said whatever it was he wanted to say, regardless of its irrelevance to the question.

You see it on live television, talk shows, and particularly in timed political debates. It happens every day. As a former political reporter, I've experienced it firsthand. I've heard some people refer to it as an answering

technique. It isn't. It's just ignoring questions and saying what you want to say.

Unfortunately, more than a handful of business executives have picked up the practice from the talk-show
politicians. For some it might work. Most of the time, it
doesn't.

A crisis is no time to ignore questions. Think about it.
If you were watching a business executive who was supposed to be telling people how he's responding to some
major crisis and he just ignored reporters' questions and
barked out prepared sound bites, what would you think?
Chances are that it wouldn't make you feel too comfortable about how that executive was handling the crisis.
You might ask yourself, "Why isn't he answering the
question? What is he trying to hide?"

Ignoring questions in a crisis will definitely send out
a message. Unfortunately, it's not the message you really
want to get across.

So how do you get your message across and still be
responsive to questions? First, make sure you know what
the message is.

Then, do what the better-trained politicians and business executives do: build a *bridge* from your response
to your message. Make no mistake: a bridge is not a way
to dodge questions, but a way to meld your message to
your answers.

> The question: Why wasn't your organization better
> prepared to deal with this crisis?

> The answer: *We don't have all of the facts at this time
> (which is the truth), but I can tell you we're doing
> everything we can right now to bring the situation
> under control, and our primary concern is to make
> sure our employees and the public are safe.*

> The question: Who do you blame for this situation?

The answer: *It's still far too early to determine the exact cause, but I can tell you we're doing everything we can at this time to bring the situation under control, and our primary concern is to make sure our employees and the public are safe.*

After trying to answer tough questions over the years, I've found that a categorical "yes" or "no" is often not much of a choice. Sometimes, you have to bridge directly to your message.

The following is one of the toughest questions an executive can be asked in a crisis where your product has been linked to injuries, illnesses, or deaths. If you say yes, no one will believe you. If you say no, you'll probably be looking for a new job.

The question: Is your product safe?

The answer: *I can only tell you that we are taking every possible precaution to assure the safety of our product.*

Another tough question that is often asked when there are real or perceived injuries or illnesses among the public as a possible result of something your company did: Will you be picking up the hospital expenses for those people who have been affected?

Chances are that you will be picking up those expenses, but in the early hours of a crisis, who knows? You want to say yes, but you have the distinct feeling that if you do say yes, that those hospital expenses will be coming out of your salary for the next 20 to 30 years.

So what is the right answer? It depends a lot on the individual company.

For many, this is an acceptable message: *It's too early to say right now exactly what action we'll be taking. Right now, our primary concern is to bring this situation*

*under control and make sure the area is safe for our
workers and people who live in the area.*

Remember, no matter what the message is, it needs to
be put into your own words and delivered in your own
style. It has to be *your* message.

We were in the living room of the gubernatorial candidate's weekend retreat. It was a small group. My videographer was with me. The candidate's wife was there also.

We had been brought in by a political consultant I
knew who thought his candidate might need some work
on his media interview skills. The consultant was right.

We had arrived the evening before. We had talked. We
did some simple interviews to evaluate his skill level.
On non-threatening questions, he wasn't bad. On tough
questions, he had some problems.

One of the toughest questions I had asked him thus
far was, "Why are you running for governor?" He really
hadn't thought of it that much so far. It was a question I
thought he ought to know by heart. How can you run for
governor without knowing why, I had to ask myself. I'm
sure voters would want to know the same thing.

We went through some other questions. I asked him the
type of questions I had asked other gubernatorial candidates when I was doing the same kind of work as a political reporter. What is it you want to do as governor? How
about education? The environment? The economy?
Taxes? I was enjoying the task. It wasn't that enjoyable
for him, however.

The next morning, I went jogging on one of the empty
dirt roads that surrounded the compound. I saw the candidate while I was out. He saw me too, I think, but neither of us said anything. Our relationship was not that of

two friends, but of a client and a consultant. He had a distrust for reporters and the fact that I had been a political reporter previously did not work in my favor. We had breakfast together and then we got back to work.

We set up the camera in a small room off the kitchen. It was where the "real" reporters would do the interview later, I figured. I wanted it to be as realistic as possible.

He appeared rather comfortable. He was dressed casually. It was Saturday. It was late October. It was cold outside. There was a crackling fire in the huge fireplace. His wife was by his side.

I began the interview.

"Why is it that you have decided to run for governor?" I asked.

His answer was along the lines we discussed the night before. It was not terribly believable, but it was better than his earlier response. I still wasn't convinced that *he* knew why he was running.

There were a few more questions. He was starting to get more comfortable. I think he was starting to enjoy it. He was perhaps too comfortable.

The line of questioning changed.

"Sir, have you ever smoked marijuana?" I asked.

There was a silence. It seemed like hours. I stopped the camera.

We talked.

Finally, we started again. I asked some other routine questions. He responded okay. But there was yet one other question I wanted to ask.

"Sir, have you ever cheated on your wife?"

Again, there was a silence. He looked at his wife. She looked at him. We stopped the camera. We took a break.

You can say the questions were out of line. You can say that whether he smoked pot as a college student or cheated on his wife as a businessman is no one else's business. But whether they are legitimate questions or not, they are going to get asked. Read your local newspaper. Watch the national news. I had asked the same or similar questions when I covered politics. Sometimes the reporter is just looking for a reaction. If you can't handle a tough, personal question, how are you going to run a major state?

The response from that would-be governor that day was almost identical to the response received from another candidate for governor years earlier when I was a political reporter and was asking the questions for real. There was speculation that the candidate was gay. If he was, he had never said anything about it. No one had written anything about it either, but the rumors persisted.

I didn't like to ask the question, but I did anyway. "There are rumors, sir, that you and another elected official are having an affair. That other official is a man. I hate to ask you this, sir, but people on the street are asking, and I'm sure the voters will ask, are you gay?" For a few seconds, I was ashamed I had even asked the question. I wasn't sure I would ever run the response, but I felt it had to be asked. It was post-Watergate. It was the time of honesty in politics. It was the time when voters—or at least the news media—felt they had the right to know everything about a candidate's personal life.

His face reddened. He became short of breath. For a while, I thought he was going to have a heart attack. His response was neither a denial nor a confirmation. He was just plain mad.

A few days later, he announced he was pulling out of the governor's race.

The point is that whether you are a candidate running for governor, or you are a plant manager speaking to reporters in the wake of a chemical spill, you need to be prepared for that question out of left field, that question you'd never expect.

> No matter how good you are, no matter who you are, you can't control the questions the media ask.

I continually ask my clients: "What's the worst question they can ask you?" I've always felt if you can handle that question, you can handle just about anything.

The candidate couldn't handle it. It wasn't the only problem with his campaign, but it was symptomatic. You might, if you're really good, be able to control your message points. You might—if you're really, really good—be able to stay in control of what you say when you respond to questions.

But no matter how good you are, no matter who you are, you can't control the questions the media ask.

"How could you let this happen?"

It's the one question students in our media training workshops say they dread the most.

It evokes emotion. It implies you did something wrong. It insinuates you somehow had the power to prevent a tragic event, yet did nothing. It's the kind of question—or accusation—one takes personally.

When it's asked by a television reporter, it can strike fear in your heart. When asked at a public meeting by a young mother concerned about the health and safety of her child because of something your company did, you feel totally helpless.

Over the years, we've heard dozens of responses to the question. There's no response that works for everyone, every time. There's no boilerplate.

The common denominator among the good responses is a conveyance of honesty and credibility. It isn't so much what a spokesperson says as much as how he or she says it.

It's the kind of question that needs a response of care and concern, as well as reassurance. It's a time for sincerity, conviction, and compassion.

In many cases, the questioner is really asking "why" something happened, or "what" caused it. If that's the case, the spokesperson might reply, "We're still trying to find out what caused it ourselves. Our main concern at this time, however, is. . . ."

Some other tough questions students say they'd like to avoid:

- Who is responsible?
- Why didn't you take precautions to prevent this from happening?
- What are you going to do about it?
- How dangerous is it?
- Who is to blame?
- Was anyone hurt or killed?
- Are you going to compensate the victims?
- When will the situation be under control?
- Can it happen again?

We continually urge people in our workshops to "stick with your message" when dealing with the news media. Part of my job in the workshops is to try to pull them away from their message. At first, it's fairly easy. Human nature is to answer a person's question. Sometimes, we try to answer questions in spite of the consequences. That can be dangerous. Eventually, however, most students learn to stay with a key message or two. By then, they may have learned the hard way what happens when they don't.

My longtime coinstructor, Tom Ryan, likes to tell the story of a workshop in Beaumont, Texas, several years ago. Tom and I were working with a chemical company, and we were training about a dozen potential spokespersons at one of the plants. Many of them were chemical engineers. All of them knew their business. They knew chemicals.

The scenario involved one of those chemicals no one wants to get close to. To call it dangerous is an understatement. Our particular scenario involved a fairly large release of the chemical. There was public concern.

Tom, playing the reporter he had been for more than 30 years before he became a media trainer, asked one of the students, "That sounds like pretty dangerous stuff. It could kill people, couldn't it?"

The student just looked at Tom and responded in his Texas drawl, "No," and there was this pregnant pause before he finished his response, ". . . not right away."

The student was honest, but he was off message. In trying to be responsive to the reporter, he had forgotten about CONTROL, CONCERN, COOPERATION, and PRAISE.

A better, yet still honest, response might have been: "It certainly can be dangerous, and that's why we're taking every precaution we can to see that the public is protected." He needed to reassure the public that actions were being taken to protect them. Had the scenario been real, those precautions would have been real too.

Some of my former students and clients continue to call me from time to time when they are getting ready for interviews. I think they know what they need to do and say, but they want a second opinion.

That was the case a few years ago when a construction company president called to tell me he would be conducting an interview with a newspaper reporter that afternoon and he wanted to go over his "nuggets" or message points.

He explained the circumstances. There was a lawsuit over one of his building projects. It was fairly complex, but it sounded like his company was innocent of any malicious wrongdoing. It sounded like they were doing the right thing.

After thinking about it for a few minutes, I called him back and advised him what I thought our key message would be. It was short and it was simple. It also was true.

"That's fine, but what if they keep asking me other questions? I can't keep saying the same thing. I'll look stupid, won't I?"

I told him he might feel stupid saying the same thing, or he could look stupid in tomorrow morning's newspaper. The choice was his. He could either stick with his message, or he could go "off message" and face the consequences.

He called me back directly after the interview. "I'm not sure," he said.

"Did you stick with the message?" I asked.

"Yeah, but I felt kind of funny. He kept asking me all kinds of questions and I kept going back to what we rehearsed."

I apologized for his anxiety, but predicted things should work out okay. The reporter would either have to run his message or not quote him at all. The reporter certainly couldn't say he refused to comment.

The next day, the paper came out and the story about his company was there. It was a straightforward story and the construction company president was quoted prominently in the story. The quote was his message.

There was another time when a network news program wanted to interview one of my clients for a story. The story involved a situation where some people within the company had worked with their competition to fix the price of a food product sold to kids in public schools. The practice was illegal. Once the company had found out about it, it had fired those people involved and cooperated with law enforcement officials in their prosecution.

The company wasn't sure at all whether it wanted to become involved in a nationally televised interview. They weren't sure anyone with the company would ever be able to put a positive message across in light of what had happened.

I began working with a senior vice president who they felt might be their best spokesperson. I talked with him at length about the situation. I read reports. I think I did my homework rather well.

We brought in a production crew for his initial interview on the subject. I wanted to see how he would do. I wanted his rehearsal to be as much like the real thing as possible. He wasn't bad, but we had yet to zero in on a message.

Before the second rehearsal, I had compiled a list of questions and suggested responses for him. I wanted him to be prepared for anything.

He looked over the list of questions. Finally, he said, "I don't believe it."

"What is it you don't believe?" I asked. "Sure, there are a lot of questions, but they might even have more. I just want you to be prepared."

"That's not it," he countered. He said he wasn't surprised that I had come up with some 65 questions on the issue.

"What I can't believe," he continued, "is that you only have three answers."

Without even thinking about it that much, I had answered all of the potential questions with one of two or three key message points. I felt no matter what the producers decided to use out of the interview, it had to carry our message.

There were three key messages:

1. What we did was wrong.

2. Those involved in it have been fired and we've taken actions to see that it won't happen again.

3. The final message was the one I knew people would demand. "I personally want to apologize to anyone who was hurt as a result of what happened."

When the story aired, the producers selected three sound bites. They were our three messages. They really had no other choice. It was all we gave them.

What do you do when a media outlet, a newspaper, a television station, a magazine is really out to get you? What do you do when they really don't care about the facts? What do you do when you're saying all the right things, but they simply are not listening?

Several options immediately come to mind. First, don't ever talk to them again. Second, call their editor, their publisher, the network. How about a retraction? What about a full-page advertisement to get your message across?

In real life, don't get paranoid. It may be just your imagination. Don't take it personally. Sure, reporters and their employers might have a preconceived idea of where they want to go with a story. And, sure, you might have little influence on changing that idea. Don't get mad. Don't get overly excited.

From experience, I can tell you that calling their bosses doesn't work very often. Publishers, editors, and news directors habitually defend their reporters. They may agree with you 100 percent that their reporter acted improperly, but they'll rarely admit it.

Demanding a retraction seldom works. You have to prove they did something wrong and they have to agree with you. That isn't likely to happen.

You can sue. But you'll probably lose. Even if the media outlet was wrong, even if they maligned you, you'll have a hard time getting a judge or jury to agree with you. And by the time they reach a verdict, no one will remember what the issue was. You've probably already lost.

So what do you do? Much of the time, nothing.

If a reporter is out to get you, you may still want to respond, but you might want to be cautious, and you might want to respond via a fax rather than a live interview.

If someone is really out to get you, you want to put out your best spokesperson. If you don't have a "best" spokesperson, then don't consent to interviews.

You can expand the coverage. It might sound stupid, but if one media outlet is out to get you, you might fare better if you get more media involved. If one media outlet is out to get you, perhaps their competitor might take the other angle. They might become your "white knight."

You can talk to the reporter. You can meet with the reporter, discuss what's going on and what is necessary to make things right.

You can stop all relations with that media outlet. This is risky, but it might work. Ignore them. Shut them out. Without you, they might not be able to get a story. Work with their competitors. Polish up your community relations.

But ultimately think: Is their story false? Are they really off base? If they are, try to correct them. Sit down and explain. If it doesn't work, then look for alternatives.

Sometimes flattery works well. I recall running into a reporter who was covering a legal hearing involving one of our clients. It was a hearing before a local judge. The issue was whether an area nursing home had taken adequate precautions to protect residents from potential harm, or whether the state should shut it down.

The story had attracted a lot of publicity. Most of it was balanced. Some of it was not. This particular reporter's coverage had been fairly one-sided, against us. It was somewhat sensational. He was portraying the nursing home management as the bad guys.

In short, his television station was hammering us.

I had come across the reporter earlier in my career when I was a political reporter, so I knew him personally, although it would have been a stretch to say we were friends.

I walked up to him and we exchanged pleasantries. We talked a bit about the "good old days" of reporting. We discussed a couple of stories we had worked on together. We talked about how things had changed a lot since those days earlier in both of our careers.

"I don't know where reporting is going these days," I said. "Some of the stuff you see on TV and in the newspapers is just so one-sided. There just doesn't seem to be any attempt to be balanced, to be fair."

He seemed to be agreeing with me. We talked about a couple of stories that were in the news at the time, totally ignoring the story he was there to cover.

At some point in the conversation, I mentioned how that was not the case in the "good old days." He agreed. I then added, "I mean, I know you'd never do anything like that."

From that moment, we started getting a fair shake from that reporter. We had played to his sense of fairness. Nothing more had to be said.

There was another reporter—an older investigative reporter who was legendary in his part of the country. He had a reputation for protecting the "little guy" and exposing corporate crooks. It's been said that he never let the facts get in the way of a good story. He was always on the side of "justice" and he had never seen a corporation he ever liked, other than possibly the corporation that owned the TV station where he was employed.

One of my clients had the misfortune to become the subject of one of his investigations. He had found wrongdoing and he felt it was his job to make it right.

The "wrongdoing" was questionable. The details aren't important. In most cities, it would never have been a story at all. But in this city, it was different.

When I got the call, the client was at wits end. How do you deal with a self-appointed prosecutor, judge, and jury? When the client said she sensed the reporter was out to get them, it was not an exaggeration. It was happening.

They had already tried reasoning, to no avail. It was time for options.

I asked the company's CEO if she was up to trying something that might seem just a little strange. At this point, I believe she would have tried anything.

I asked her to call the reporter, identify herself as the president and CEO of the company he was lambasting. But rather than complain, I wanted her to thank him for bringing this issue to her attention.

"This is not the way we conduct business," she would

tell him. "Once we became aware of what happened, we immediately took actions to see that it was halted. We just won't tolerate that kind of activity," she would continue.

She had appealed to his ego. She had let him win. He had corrected injustice once again. The story ended.

What she had said was true. Her company didn't tolerate "that kind of activity." It never had.

From time to time, I'm asked how or why I made the move from covering politics to opening a crisis management firm. Occasionally I'll joke about how moving from politics to crisis management wasn't that much of a stretch. Quite often, politics was a crisis in the making. Think about the Clinton administration.

But it goes much farther than that, and it really didn't involve politics.

I was on one of those "nonpolitical" assignments when I was a reporter in Chicago. I had been sent to Kansas City to cover a story, and my job was to interview the chief executive of a major organization. I had set up the interview with the executive's secretary. I told her basically what I needed and the kind of story I was doing. I figured she'd pass it on to the executive.

A day or so later, I walked into the executive's office. I sat down in a chair and opened my notepad. I was prepared to move on with the interview.

Following some cordialities, he asked, "So what is it you want to talk about?"

He clearly had no idea why I was there. He was going into an important interview with a major media outlet, and he didn't have a clue what he was going to say. To say he was unprepared was an understatement.

He had underrated the importance as well as the danger of dealing with the news media. He had no idea what his message was because he had no idea what the subject was.

I almost felt sorry for him. Almost.

He should have known better. But then, I'm sure no one had ever told him about dealing with the news media. He had figured the same skills that had moved him to the top of his organization would help him through an interview. I'm convinced he just thought he could wing it. It was a dangerous assumption on his part.

I left that interview without much of a story. I'd get my sound bites, my nuggets, my quotes somewhere else. But I did leave that interview with the seed of a new business. I wondered how many other business executives were going into media interviews so unprepared.

The answer, I found, was scary.

SPOKESPERSONS

In a crisis, selecting the right spokesperson can be one of the most important decisions any crisis team can make.

Even if you do everything right—even if you have all the right messages—it means little if the person who serves as your spokesperson isn't credible.

Credibility is the most important quality in a spokesperson. It is far more important that charisma. It beats "slick" any day of the week. If the spokesperson isn't believable, it doesn't matter what he or she says.

In a crisis, the best spokesperson is generally someone local, someone with authority, and someone who has the skills to get their message across.

In the majority of crises, the best spokesperson is rarely a public relations executive or the CEO.

Selecting the right spokesperson can be one of the most important decisions you can make in a crisis.

Public relations executives are best used as conduits to spokespersons. They can keep the media abreast of what's happening, but only in rare circumstances should they serve as the primary spokesperson in a major crisis. It's not that they're not qualified. They may be almost too qualified. It's more of a credibility issue. In a crisis, the public—and the media—would probably prefer hearing from someone in charge, someone local and someone responsible.

The CEO may well be the company's best spokesperson, but only in situations that eliminate most others from consideration. It also depends on the size of the company. In a company with 100 employees, the CEO might be the exact person. At General Motors, however, you might want to think about it.

No matter whom you use as your spokesperson, it has to make sense. Don't go with someone because it's their job or because they're good, but because they're the best person for that particular situation.

As a general rule, the best spokesperson is the highest-ranking—or one of the highest-ranking—officials at the site where the crisis takes place. That might be a general manager or plant manager for larger corporations. That's why plant managers make up a large percentage of the people we train for spokesperson roles.

But title alone isn't enough to qualify someone for the spokesperson role. Even if you have the title of president before your name, the title doesn't mean much if you can't communicate. Therefore, the spokesperson's qualifications in dealing with the news media are a key concern in the selection process.

> In a crisis, the public—and the media—would probably prefer hearing from someone in charge, someone local and someone responsible.

The issue was environmental justice. It involved a chemical plant in Louisiana. Local residents said the plant wasn't hiring minorities from the neighborhood.

A large PR firm from New York had been brought in to help the company. Our firm was asked to help prepare their spokesperson.

The plant manager was a local guy. He had grown up in the area. He had graduated from Louisiana State University. He spoke the local language. But he was white.

The PR firm wanted an African-American spokesperson. They wanted more. They wanted an African-American spokesperson who was female and who was an officer in the company.

When no one fit the description, they started shopping around. They found a fairly high-ranking female executive who was also an African American. She was smart. She was attractive. She was the kind of person you'd expect to see on the cover of *CEO* magazine some day. I had known her for several years and I knew she was at the top of her game. I had worked with her before in preparing her for news media encounters. She was good. Reporters liked her. There was one problem. She had nothing to do with the chemical side of the business. She was not from Louisiana and had never been to the plant.

It didn't matter. "Just train her," I was told.

She was reluctant to take on her new role as the newest vice president for the chemical company. We talked for a while and then we turned on the video camera and began our first interview.

My first question: "How long have you worked for this particular organization?" There was a pause. She was nervous, and being nervous wasn't one of her traits. She could handle just about anything, but she couldn't handle that question. She had exactly one day of seniority with the business she was now being asked to represent.

"Why were you named a vice president of this organization?" I asked. "And just when were you named?" She stammered a bit and then asked for a break.

She obviously could not be their spokesperson. She was a reluctant volunteer from the beginning. She knew exactly why she was being used, but she was a loyal employee. Eventually she realized the best thing she could do for the company was to say "no." We ultimately used the local plant manager instead.

Neither the media nor the public are blind. They can see right through charades where spokespersons are selected solely because of their race or gender.

We were working with a nursing home that had been charged with neglecting its patients, or "residents" as they are referred to by nursing home officials.

I met with executives from the company that managed the home to discuss strategies on dealing with the news media. They weren't overly cooperative. They seemed to think if they paid me enough money, I could make their problem go away. I wish it were that easy. We got down to the subject of who should speak for the nursing home in question. I thought it should be someone in management, possibly an officer in the management company or the home's administrator. They thought differently.

They wanted their public relations person to handle the media.

I went along with them for the time being. I didn't have much choice.

I started working with the PR person. We went to the home and we were going through some mock interviews. It was apparent to me that this approach was not going to work out the way I wanted it to.

We were in a small office at the nursing home and conducting yet another mock interview to prepare him to face the real news media. We had lights on the camera. As the interview got underway, he seemed to have the right answers, but they weren't particularly believable. In retrospect, I don't think he believed them either. Then he began to sweat.

I found it hard to take him as a credible spokesperson when there was this bead of sweat dripping across his face. No one else would either.

Both of us agreed, there was probably a better spokesperson for this issue within the organization. Again, we thought possibly the administrator, the head nurse, somebody who was directly involved in patient care. We were overruled, however, by management.

I was on the road in Texas when the TV station called and wanted to interview someone about the situation. They had already talked to the family of the nursing home resident. They just wanted the nursing home's side. The PR guy told me he had agreed to talk to them. He'd call me later and tell me how it went. I wished him luck. I knew he'd need it.

That evening, I was in my hotel room when he called. He seemed a little shaken. It was apparent that he didn't think the interview went as well as he wanted it to. He told me what he said to the reporter. He had stuck to his message points, he said. That was good. But there was more.

When the *real* interview took place, it was in that same small office where we had practiced. He was seated behind a desk. It was a small desk. It wasn't his desk, and he looked uncomfortable.

It was the same room I had suggested we never use because it was too small and the light on the camera would generate too much heat. As a general rule, I prefer not to tape interviews in offices. They always seem too sterile. Then there was the desk. It just served as a barrier between him and the people who would be watching him on television. It was like he had to be protected from the television viewers, or worse, that he was trying to look important. Behind someone else's desk in someone else's tiny office, he looked like one of those TV commercials you see on weekend afternoons. Only this one was a very bad commercial.

Even though it was January, even though we were in the Midwest, I had suggested we conduct the interview outside the nursing home, perhaps in the parking lot with the building behind him. It was an attractive building. It conveyed a subtle message that the home was nice, and that nice homes like this one don't hurt people. It was cold in the parking lot, but it was better than that office. I wasn't there that day, however, and the PR guy opted for the office anyway.

When I returned to my office, I was handed a videotape of his television interview. There was the obligatory "standup" in front of the home where the reporter told viewers what had happened. Then they cut to the interview. Looking back, I don't even remember what the reporter asked, or even the PR guy's response. No one else would remember either. It would make no difference what he said. As the videographer zoomed in for a closeup, all you could focus on was that bead of sweat rolling down the spokesperson's face. At this point, it was clear no one was paying any attention at all to what he was saying.

Shortly afterwards, I resigned the account. It was clear we'd never be able to work together. They ultimately hired a PR firm with "connections" in state government. They wanted someone to *fix* the situation for them. They had no intention of fixing it themselves.

It was a different time and a different nursing home, but the situation was much the same. Someone had died. The family blamed the nursing home and the state was investigating.

When I took the call from the attorney representing the home, he suggested there was probably nothing anyone could do at this point. He was just trying to make the best of a bad situation. He even called it "damage control." He knew they were going down, he just didn't know how far. We weren't the first firm he had talked to.

The others had basically told him the nursing home would probably be closed. It was not a good situation.

A local television station had been hammering the home bad. It had been going on for some time, but until now it was just the one station covering the story. They had interviewed family members with tears in their eyes. It was pretty emotional—the kind of story TV producers love. I've seen variations of it on other TV stations across the country.

The station had asked to talk to someone from the home, but they had denied all requests. They were afraid that things might become even worse.

The lawyer wanted me to meet with the president of the company that ran the home. She was a registered nurse turned businesswoman, and she had done rather well in the nursing home industry. Today, however, she was in trouble and she knew it.

My initial impression was not what I was expecting. She didn't come across as a hard-nosed CEO, but a disheveled woman under a lot of pressure. I'm not sure of the last time she had slept, but it was clear it had been a while. She seemed exhausted. She wasn't the kind of woman you would automatically want to place in front of television cameras to defend a besieged nursing home. But there was something about her I liked: her smile. I felt others would like her too, given the chance. It was Friday evening.

She had been living at a hotel near the nursing home for more than a week, and she looked like she had been living out of suitcases or her car. I asked her to take Saturday off, get some rest, forget about work. I suggested she go shopping, buy some new clothes, and visit a local spa where she could get her hair done and perhaps get a massage. We would meet again, I told her, on Sunday morning. The news conference, I suggested, would be held on Monday. I don't know why she followed my

orders, but she did. I think she really wanted a break.
She certainly needed one. The crisis would still be there
on Sunday.

When we met Sunday morning, I knew we had a lot of
work to do. We went through all sorts of questions and
started working on message points that we wanted to get
across. I wanted to play the "nurse card" with her. She
was genuinely concerned about the residents at the home,
and I knew she could get that across if we could raise her
comfort level. I suggested she just needed to be herself. I
was counting an awful lot on that smile, I told her.

We worked on an opening statement and continued
practicing how she would answer the tough questions we
both knew would be asked.

On Monday, I alerted the media that we would be holding a news conference at the nursing home to respond to
the charges of neglect. Every media outlet in town
turned out for it. It was no longer a story to be covered
by just one television station. It was a gamble on my part,
but I didn't think we'd get far working with a station
that had already determined the nursing home was
guilty and was just waiting for a judge to hand down the
verdict. With enough coverage, I thought we had a better
chance of getting our story—the full story—before the
public.

As she began addressing the group of reporters, she
was visibly nervous, but she continued. She was wringing
her hands together, but the smile was still there. Her concern for the residents was still there. The media liked her.

That evening, the news conference played out on all
the local television stations. She was doing well. She was
more than holding her own.

At the end of the story on one station, the two
coanchors were bantering back and forth the way they
do. They were commenting on the news conference and
their reporter's coverage that day. "It's just kind of hard

to believe the charges," one anchor said. "They seem so nice." At that exact moment, I knew we had turned the corner. I knew we'd win.

When we conduct media training or "spokesperson" training workshops around the country, there's a tendency among some participants to try to fit the mold of what they think a typical spokesperson should be. The problem is that there is no mold, or at least there shouldn't be. Spokespersons should not be products of media training workshops; they should be real people.

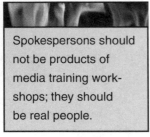

Spokespersons should not be products of media training workshops; they should be real people.

Our typical class size is about eight students. I tell students that at the end of the day, we'll probably have eight totally different approaches to handling interviews. Some students will be tough. Some will be authoritative. Some will be extremely believable. They hopefully should all be carrying the same key message, but they should do it in their own style. It's okay, I tell them, to be yourself.

If you can get your message across and you can do it in a credible fashion, I don't care how you do it.

This is not an acting class, I tell them. There are too many unemployed actors already. This class is designed to increase your comfort level in conducting interviews. This class hopefully will show you how to get your message across.

Throughout our workshops, we show videotaped examples of spokespersons answering tough questions. Some are staged, many are real. Several examples in our workbook show how you can answer tough questions.

We develop others on the spot as we work our way through various crisis scenarios. But all those examples on tape, in the book, and the ones we develop together are just that; they're examples. If you try to repeat the same phrase in a workshop, or in real life, it would be acting. It would be fake. It would not be credible. It would not work.

Most of the time in our workshops, we develop the key message points as a group. They are usually similar from one class to another, but they are never the same. As we list them all on the board or flipchart pad, I try to ask students: Is there anyone in this class who doesn't believe what we have up here? Is there anyone who wouldn't be comfortable expressing this message? Because if there is, I warn, then this cannot be your message.

If you don't believe it, then you can't say it—at least not with conviction.

We found that out in New Mexico during a training session. We had just completed our first round of interviews and my associate, Tom Ryan, was critiquing one of the students on his performance. I don't recall what the man did right or wrong, but Tom felt he could stand some improvement.

The man, in the most polite way he knew how, fired back to Tom with a comment that forever changed my attitude toward media training.

"Mr. Ryan," he said, "I can't help it. I am who I am."

CHAPTER

9

MOCK DISASTERS

It had been less than three months since the events of
September 11, 2001, and nuclear plants across the
country were on high alert. A congressman and his press
aide were on site to get a firsthand view of how the plant
was prepared to respond to potential terrorist attacks.
An OSHA inspector as well as an inspector from the
Nuclear Regulatory Commission were both on site for
routine business.

It was precisely 8:45 A.M. when the explosion took
place on the northeast side of the plant. You could smell
what appeared to be chlorine gas coming from the
scene. Emergency personnel were dispatched.

Preliminary reports were that six workers were injured. At least two were missing. Emergency procedures were under way. Residents closest to the plant
were evacuated by local authorities. Others were asked
to remain in their homes.

Within 30 minutes, the first reporters were beginning to arrive at an off-site facility now being utilized as an emergency news media center. More reporters would arrive soon.

Fifteen minutes later, a local radio station received a call from a man who claimed he was responsible for the blast. He tells them he has 12 hostages being held at gunpoint. The interview is aired live. The reporter calls the plant, telling them what he has learned and offers to play the tape of the interview.

As the "head count" continues at the plant, security determines 13 people cannot be accounted for. One of them is an aide to the congressman.

At 9:45 A.M., a local television station receives a cellular call from one of their former reporters, now the press aide for a congressman. He claims he's being held hostage at a nuclear facility. There are others.

It was a complex scenario, and it was all make-believe.

There was no explosion. There were no hostages. It was a test of the plant's ability to respond to a crisis in what has become known in America as the era of "post 9-11."

It was tough. There were reporters and television cameras. The citizens' hotline was flooded with calls from local residents who wanted to know what to do in this emergency. Relatives called the center for information on their loved ones who worked at the plant.

Spokespersons and public affairs representatives were forced to respond to the news media and the public even though they had little information to give them. In that regard, this exercise—this mock disaster—was very real.

If crisis management training and media training are intended to prepare corporations for what to do and what to say when a crisis happens, then mock disasters are the test to see what they learned.

To be successful, a mock disaster must be challenging, but not impossible.

Most of the mock disasters we conduct for clients run their course in just two or three hours. Unfortunately, four, five, or even six months or more may be needed to prepare for one.

> Mock disasters are simply an extension of crisis management training. They are the final test before the real event.

The secret to creating mock disasters is to know ahead of time what you want to learn from them. You have to have preset objectives, and there must be a way of grading performance. You have to know what went right and what went wrong. Mock disasters are simply an extension of crisis management training. They are the final test before the real event.

You can learn a lot from a mock disaster. That's the reason for their existence. You learn what you do right and you learn what you do wrong. Sometimes you learn you don't know half as much as you think you do. That's one reason mock disasters can be painful. Learning isn't always fun. It isn't always easy.

In one mock disaster, we found security was so lax at a hospital that reporters with television cameras had free reign of the facility. They could move floor-to-floor, interview staff members, nurses, doctors, and even patients. Imagine what a terrorist could do.

The crisis team's meeting room was adjacent to the media center. As a result, reporters simply waited for people to enter or exit the room and then "ambushed" them without warning.

In order to be successful, a mock disaster must be challenging, but not impossible.

So many people were talking to reporters and providing information that stories varied greatly, depending on the last person you talked to. There was a lot of misinformation being handed out as "official" statements.

In trying to get a quick grasp on the situation, the first crisis team leaders forgot to contact the public affairs officer or the president. Whoops!

Switchboards were overwhelmed. Security was overwhelmed. The hospital was overwhelmed.

After the drill was critiqued and everyone had an opportunity to offer their thoughts on what happened, we issued a final report with more than 100 recommendations for improvement. It was a major drill. It was an expensive drill. And the hospital had taken it seriously. They used it as a learning experience. Management ultimately addressed every single recommendation.

We conducted additional drills for that hospital over the years. In each one, the hospital became better and better.

Mock disasters don't have to be terribly expensive. They don't have to be terribly complex. It's best to decide first what you want to find out as a result of the mock disaster, and how much you want to spend. You can then build a mock disaster to meet your objectives and your budget.

One of the more elaborate mock disasters we ever staged was for a chemical company that wanted to involve the people at one of its plants, along with top executives at headquarters. The two complexes were hundreds of miles apart. They said they wanted a mock disaster that was serious enough that—if it really happened—it would force the involvement of the company president. They said they wanted a mock disaster that was so tough, their people would barely be able to respond to it. At the end of the mock disaster, they said, they wanted everyone to breathe a sigh of relief that it was over. They knew exactly what they wanted, but they just weren't sure how to make it happen.

I asked for a six-month lead time to prepare. We were given a little less than three months. I visited the plant site and met with some of their emergency management personnel. One would be assigned to work with me to develop the scenario and help implement it once it was developed. He would not be involved in the actual exercise, nor would he divulge any information about the exercise to others. Once we were given the go-ahead to stage the exercise, only a handful of people would be kept abreast of what was happening, or even when it would happen.

We started first with a scenario that would be suffi-
ciently disastrous to accomplish the company's goals. It
would be a flaming barge, filled with chemicals that ultimately could explode. It would take place on the river
in a metropolitan area.

Once we agreed on the scenario, I began the task of creating a timeline for the events and ultimately a script.
Putting together a realistic mock disaster is somewhat
like writing a screenplay. The events are scripted to pre-
cise times. Unfortunately, those people reacting to our
events don't have a script. That's the test and that's the
one factor we have no control over. We only create the
disaster; we don't solve it for them.

For this particular disaster, we decided to utilize no
less than five television crews, along with a dozen other
mock reporters. All of our reporters were "regulars"
who had participated in our mock disasters in the past.
All of them were former broadcast journalists. We con-
tracted for the news photographers and TV cameras. We
also utilized the services of "citizens" and public officials who would be played by our regulars with mock
disaster experience.

Since an event of the type we were staging would involve police and fire authorities, we brought them into
our mock disaster. They were given no detailed information on the event in advance. They were not told when it
would happen until an hour before.

Those participants in our disaster were only told there
would be one during an approximate one-month period.
The date and time was kept secret. Our only consideration for timing was to make sure the company's CEO
would be in the country when it took place.

Our mock news media came into town the evening
before the exercise. We would operate out of a nearby
hotel, using it as our staging area. Special phone lines
were installed for outgoing and incoming calls. Every-

one was given their own script that they would follow the next morning. They only knew their part of the scenario. Only two of us knew the entire scenario.

The next morning, we made calls approximately 15 minutes prior to the drill to tell telephone operators that a drill would be taking place that day. All calls regarding the drill would be identified as such. Signs were placed in areas where confusion by the drill might cause a public concern. We didn't want this to become a "War of the Worlds" situation. It's easy for that to happen.

About one minute prior to the drill, I made some specific calls to alert people that the drill was on. After that, it would be difficult to make any changes, although we were in constant contact by cell phone and walkie-talkie.

Within 15 minutes, emergency responders and crisis team members were totally involved. An emergency operations center was set up. Corporate was notified. Within 20 minutes, reporters were on the scene. Television coverage had begun.

Within three hours, it was over.

The entire event was videotaped. We had news cameras covering every angle of the event in both cities. We had one "quiet" camera inside the Emergency Operations Center to record actions of the responders. It would be important for the critique later.

We took more than 14 hours of videotape and edited it into an approximate 20-minute documentary that showed the disaster drill from beginning to end. The video was better than any written or verbal report we could put together. The depiction of the drill was very real. Had it been real, I'm convinced we would have won an Emmy.

It had been an exhaustive drill. It had been an expensive drill. But it was a good drill that had met the company's objectives.

At the end of it all, almost everyone was sighing relief. They were glad it was over.

We were working on a mock disaster at an oil refinery. The scenario had already been decided. It was to be a tornado. It was to be a really bad tornado. It would not only impact the refinery, but the town as well. It would not only involve the oil company, but local public officials.

It was the company's idea to ask the local mayor, police chief, fire chief, and a handful of others to participate.

As part of the preparation, the company asked if we could take some of the city officials through a brief media training session. It was a good idea. I doubt very many public officials in small communities ever get to experience the media training that some of the larger corporations do. The oil company kept at arms length during the training. We conducted it at City Hall. No representatives from the company were present.

A few days later, when the mock disaster took place, the mayor, the police chief, and the fire chief all participated. They assumed leading roles at news conferences and in making the kinds of decisions that affected the entire community. It was the way it would have been in real life.

The mayor did an excellent job as chief spokesperson. He took his training seriously and he applied the training in the mock disaster.

After it was over, I had an opportunity to talk with him privately. He said he had always felt the refinery officials were pretty well prepared to deal with a crisis, but until that day, he didn't know how well prepared they were. He was impressed with what he had seen that day. It was time well spent.

We received a call from a hospital not long ago that wanted to conduct a mock disaster to test its senior management. They didn't have a lot of time or a lot of money. The date had already been set.

I suggested a sort of "table top" exercise in which we would put together a scenario they could react to and do it as part of their already preset meeting. The exercise would take approximately two hours and would involve all senior staff people. I would put together the scenario and assemble a small crew of about four people to carry it out. They would provide some of their own people to work with my crew.

As with most mock disasters, it took longer than we thought to develop the scenario. There were new twists and turns being injected. But it was a good scenario that would involve all aspects of senior management, including the CEO. Did I mention that it might have been the most complex scenario I've ever been involved with? Actually, it was several scenarios all wrapped up into one mock disaster. Ultimately, we were able to weave them together in a script and timetable that made sense. At least it made sense to us. We only hoped it would make sense to those people who would be subjected to it.

The event went off without a hitch. We had three on-scene reporters and one photographer. The total cost was about the same as a media training workshop. It was a fraction of what a more elaborate drill would have cost, but it worked, and it met their objectives.

COMMUNITY RELATIONS

S ometimes you never know how much you need community relations until you realize you don't have any.

That was the case for a printing facility in suburban St. Louis in the mid-1990s. The scene was City Council chambers. It was crowded and the crowd was angry. The issue was odor, or at least that's what officials with the printing company thought it was. It turned out to be a whole lot more.

That's the problem with odors. There's often a lot more behind them than meets the nose. In this case, a close examination found that the odor was caused by mercaptan, that ingredient that gives odorless natural gas its distinctive smell. To say that a little bit of mercaptan goes a long, long way is an understatement. And in this case, there was more than just a little bit of it.

There was another problem with mercaptan. A lot of people were convinced it would cause serious health problems, including cancer. And the crowd at City Hall didn't care much whether there were only minute trace amounts of it in the air. For most people, there is no safe level for something they think might cause cancer.

No one is sure when the odor/cancer issue really started, but by the time the company went to the city to get permission to expand its facility, it had become one of the top controversies government officials had ever had to face.

Some people trace the roots of the controversy to a quaint restaurant where several of the town's leading women would gather for tea from time to time. The restaurant or tea room had the misfortune of being

When reporters are already at your doorstep, it's a little too late to be thinking of putting together a community relations plan.

directly next to the printing facility's exhaust fan. Most of the odors from the plant were vented directly toward the restaurant.

That particular side of the plant boasted a rather unsightly wall with weeds and a rusting chain-link fence as the only separator. Not only were patrons of the restaurant subjected to an odor from the plant, but an unsightly view as well.

Then there was the traffic pattern around the plant. Employees were said to make a race track out of local streets on their way to and from work. That statement was only a slight exaggeration.

A similar story repeats itself across America all the time. People aren't even aware of the industrial facility until there's a problem. By then, it's a bit late to do anything about it. Companies should really give more attention to community relations before there is a problem.

In this case, the problem was rather intense before the company felt it needed to do something. A vote before the council that would allow an expansion of the plant to put in new environmental controls was about to take place. Without the city's approval, the plant would not meet federal mandates. It would close. For local residents, the choice was beginning to lean toward getting rid of the plant, period.

Fixing the problem was not easy, but it wasn't that difficult either. First, you had to put yourself in the neighbors' shoes. You had to see the facility the way they did. It wasn't pretty . . . and it did stink.

Early recommendations following our initial visit there: Relocate the exhaust fan immediately. Stop venting odors into the adjoining restaurant. Beyond that, use some common sense.

We asked the owners and patrons of the restaurant to help us choose a decorative fence and landscaping that would shield them from the plant. It wasn't that expensive, but it was long overdue. We also repainted the side of the building facing the restaurant. It was cosmetic, but it was important. We wanted something immediate and we wanted something visible.

Beyond that, we replaced the aging signs around the plant with attractive new ones. Signs also went up warning employees to slow down.

It was decided to switch processes at the plant that would change the types of chemicals used. It would get rid of the odor and the possible link to cancer. It wasn't cheap, but it was necessary.

We held community meetings with our neighbors. We invited them to visit the plant in small, intimate groups. We told them what we did, and what we were doing. They listened. We listened. We also met individually with local community leaders.

We were fortunate that we had a new general manager who had not been with the organization when the problem began. He could not be blamed for the problem, but he would be held responsible for solving it. He was our lead spokesperson before the council, at community meetings, and with the news media. He adapted to the role well. People seemed to like him. More importantly, they believed him.

The immediate issue was ultimately resolved. But in retrospect, there should never have been an issue. Had the plant's earlier management opened their eyes earlier to the community that surrounded them, there might never have been a problem. Many of the problems the plant had to deal with were created because it failed to recognize it was part of a community and it had to get along with its neighbors. The company couldn't ignore the community without paying the consequences.

A few months earlier in southern Ohio, a community was trying to close down a local dairy because it made too much noise. At least that's what company officials were being told when that issue came before City Council. As usual, there was more to the story.

In this case, the dairy was built during the 1950s in what was then a relatively remote part of the city. As the years passed, people began building their homes almost next door. By the late 1980s, homeowners began to resent their neighbor. The neighbor, they said, made too much noise and was therefore in violation of the city's new noise ordinance. The plant had two choices: get a variance, or stop the noise. If it didn't do something, it would close.

Until this point, the dairy plant had simply coexisted with its neighbors. Most of the time, it had ignored them. It could do so no longer.

The weekend before I was to meet with the plant's management team, I made an unannounced visit to the community. I drove around the subdivision that now surrounded the plant and tried to envision what it would be like to live next to the dairy. I had gotten out of the car and was walking near the plant when I ran into a local resident. She asked why I was there, and I told her the company had asked me to check out some complaints. She gave me an ear full.

The next day, I met with the plant's management and told them of my encounter and my own impression of the plant and its surroundings. I told them we had to make noticeable improvements if we were to alter public opinion in the community. I suggested we start immediately.

When it finally decided to confront the issue, the plant's management was urged to be straightforward with its employees about how serious the issue was and how management planned to deal with the problem. The company made a concentrated effort to cut down on noise. The effort was successful, but not quite successful enough to pass the city's noise ordinance. It still needed a variance.

In talking with neighbors, the problem turned out to be more than just noise. One of the plant's high-powered lights along the fence line glared directly into one of its neighbor's bedroom windows. That was fairly easily remedied. We shielded the light.

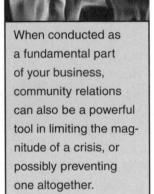

When conducted as a fundamental part of your business, community relations can also be a powerful tool in limiting the magnitude of a crisis, or possibly preventing one altogether.

We also changed delivery and pickup patterns to cut down on noise. Highly visible signage was placed throughout the plant property reminding employees and visitors that being noisy wasn't neighborly. Suggestion boxes were placed in employee gathering places. Employees used them and several were ultimately used in what eventually became known in Ohio as "the quiet campaign." Employees were no longer part of the problem; they were part of the solution.

Through the local newspaper, company officials also let the community know how much they contributed to the community in payrolls and taxes. It was significant. Until then, no one knew of the plant's contributions.

Letters were written to the local newspapers. Reporters were kept abreast of all new developments. Spokespersons were selected, coached, and used on local television.

Ultimately, the variance was passed. The plant remained open. The entire effort had taken just over a month and the overall costs were minimal. The savings to the company in not having to close the plant were estimated in the millions.

In my experience, I've found community relations to be a powerful tool in managing crisis situations and particularly in trying to recover from a major crisis. When conducted as a fundamental part of your business, community relations can also be a powerful tool in limiting the magnitude of a crisis, or possibly preventing one altogether.

In a small community in northern South Carolina, there's a processing facility that manufactures a synthetic, pow dered "cream" used to flavor coffee.

A few years ago, more than a bit of the product was blown out the drying tower in the plant, and for a few moments, the community found itself with what appeared to be a man-made snow. Unfortunately, when this "snow" came into contact with the dew on automobiles or aluminum-sided homes, it turned into something that more resembled white cement. A local newspaper writer had a field day with the story. It was picked up by wire services and it ran internationally. The plant's parent company was not particularly amused. Neither were environmental officials in South Carolina. Those directly impacted by the problem were far from happy.

Stopping the problem was not easy, but it was being done. A larger issue was the problem within the community. Wounds needed to be healed. Impacted residents wanted more than their car washed for free. They wanted resolution. The problem in the small community went all the way to the statehouse in Columbia.

After meeting with local plant officials and getting some idea of the problem they were facing, we began doing research on the community. We quietly conducted a survey of the community, talking with local government and civic leaders. We wanted to get a pulse of the community and find out where the plant and its people stood there because they seemed to be invisible. The plant had been in the community for years, but no one ever mentioned it, unless prompted. Then, they only recalled problems, not contributions.

We talked with employees. We talked with neighbors. We talked with state officials. We found another economics-related issue. The community was especially proud of its history and felt it had a future with tourism, but it needed help. That was the peg that began a successful community relations program.

We asked employees not only to get involved in the program, but to help shape it. If the program was to work, it had to be their program, not something a consultant invented and forced down their throats.

The final result was a multifaceted program that—among other things—involved volunteers from the plant serving coffee at a state welcome center along I-77. When we first started, we were told employees would never support it. After the first event received significant television coverage, we were swamped with more volunteers than we needed. We had to have waiting lists.

We also "adopted" a stretch of highway and kept it clean. And we erected a billboard welcoming visitors to the historic town. The highway gave employees a way to give back to the community. The billboard was visible.

You look back and you can say all those activities never eliminated the "white cement." They didn't. But they did help move public opinion to our side and allowed us to do what we needed to do. It helped create the kind of environment that made solving the problem possible. It also fostered morale among employees and created a bond between the plant, its immediate neighbors, and their community.

In community relations—as in crisis management—it's important to not try to create a solution before you know what the real problem is. In almost every case I've been involved with, the issue was always broader than perceived by those people closest to it.

Don't be afraid to go out into the community and ask questions. It can be done openly—or discreetly—but it has to be done. Find out what the community thinks of you. Do they even know you exist? What have you ever done for them? Anything?

I normally start with leading government officials, business leaders, and even local newspaper editors. I ask them who they think are the opinion shapers in the community and I move on from there. Eventually, you get an idea of what the community thinks. It's much faster and probably just as effective as any quantitative survey. It's usually far less expensive and it can build goodwill in the process just by talking to the right people.

Community relations is more than making annual contributions to local charities. You can't purchase goodwill with a donation. It does not have to be expensive. It has to be earned. Some of the best programs carry modest price tags. The test is not how much it costs, but whether it works. Does it accomplish what you set out to do? Do you know what you set out to do? Is there a purpose? What is your goal?

> Community relations is more than making annual contributions to local charities. You can't purchase goodwill with a donation.

Community relations programs have to be inspired and maintained locally. Employees are essential to their success. If the employees aren't involved, the program is doomed to failure from the start. Everyone wins with a good community relations program that truly involves employees. And don't say they won't become involved. If it's their program, they will.

There's a tendency in corporate America to hire consultants, let them put together a community relations program, and let them implement it. Let me tell you from experience that it doesn't work. The consultants can only help you build a program. You have to make it work.

Community relations is not a one-time thing. It has to be ongoing. It has to be constantly reviewed, updated, and reinvented. The real test of a community relations program is whether it will pass the test of time.

REPUTATION MANAGEMENT

It can take decades for an organization to build a good reputation, yet it can be destroyed in just a few hours.

Newspapers and television newscasts carry stories almost daily about companies that have been severely tarnished or destroyed by a crisis that was not properly managed. Whether the industry is automobiles, hamburgers, or pharmaceuticals, a company is never stronger than its reputation.

When you go to the heart of crisis management communications, the goal of just about every strategy ultimately is to preserve the image or the reputation of the organization involved.

Reputation management and crisis management are intertwined. A company that doesn't care about crisis management doesn't really care about its reputation. Companies who take crisis management seriously embark on whatever actions are necessary to protect that reputation.

The people who go through our media training workshops tell us they want to avoid "looking bad" in the news media. More importantly, however, they express their concern that their statements to the news media might make their *company* look bad. Our workshop attendees are going through media training to help protect their company's reputation, not their own.

> When our clients confront the news media in a crisis situation, they don't do it because they have to. They do it because they are concerned about their company's image.

When our clients confront the news media in a crisis situation, they don't do it because they have to. They do it because they are concerned about their company's image. They are afraid of what people might think if the company didn't respond to the issue at hand.

Advertising, public relations, community relations, and good business practices are important in managing corporate reputations. But when the chips are down, crisis management is imperative.

When it comes to protecting a company's reputation, never underestimate the power of disgruntled employees or ex-employees. Such people might feel the need for revenge or be attempting to correct perceived wrongdoings. Whatever the motivation, their actions can be strong enough to bring even the largest of organizations to their proverbial knees.

A strike back at a present or former employer can take many forms. Sometimes people make threats, which may or may not be carried out. People with grudges sometimes target individuals within an organization or go after the organization and its reputation. By destroying an organization's reputation, people can destroy the organization itself, or at least severely cripple its ability to function normally.

That's what began unfolding during the summer of 2000 when a former high-ranking executive with a not-for-profit organization began a crusade to destroy his former employer.

It began with a call from a New York-based reporter who was following up on an anonymous, five-page memo he had received charging the organization with gross abuses. The memo's author backed up the allegation with a detailed outline that gave names, dates, and specifics of how the organization had supposedly cheated its members out of hundreds of thousands of dollars.

The memo purported to reveal a pattern of fraud, deceit, and corporate arrogance that its author claimed had seldom been documented in the charitable world. The reporter had been sent the information, the memo said, because the public "deserved the right to know" about it.

The reporter was unsure about how much credibility could be placed in a memo that, after all, had been sent to him anonymously. Still, he felt an obligation to at least investigate it. The reporter called his contact at the organization, who bought some time by stating he would check it out. The allegations alarmed the person inside the organization, but he didn't show it. The contact obtained a copy of the memo outlining the allegations.

Although the letter was anonymous, the organization's leaders had no doubt where it came from. The style of writing, the choice of particular words, and certain knowledge of highly confidential information led management to believe that the author could be only one person. Proving it, however, would probably be impossible.

When the organization called me, they had yet to respond to the reporter's request for information. At this point, they weren't sure what they needed to do, but it was clear they were mad.

My travel schedule didn't allow me to meet with the organization immediately, but within minutes—via conference calls, emails, and fax machines—we began our plan of attack.

After reading the infamous memo, my first question was to ask if any of the allegations were true. Although the allegations were based on very real events, it was the author's interpretation of those events that made them scandalous. The organization was convinced that while it was not perfect, it certainly wasn't the type of organization described in the memo.

The nonprofit responded that the allegations were unfounded, but that if the reporter wanted more information, just let them know. The waiting period had now begun.

The organization went through every single allegation in the memo and put together responses. We also began a Q&A based on the memo. If reporters began asking questions, we wanted to be able to deliver answers.

Meanwhile, the battle lines grew. Some key contributors to the organization were receiving calls about the memo. Employees were beginning to ask questions. Even if the memo was never officially published, knowledge of it was becoming widespread. It was only a matter of time before members would be calling with questions about the allegations.

We met personally with key executives of the organization and explained the situation, trying to be as honest as possible. Employees were all given basic information about the charges. A memo also went out to members. The details were never mentioned because we felt that would only give the allegations credibility, which we wanted to avoid at all cost.

Our strong suit was that the organization had developed a solid reputation over the years as a premier group and was in an enviable position in the not-for-profit world. Long before the memo had been written, I had been proud to be associated with the group. I still feel that way, as do its members. I felt that to even hint that the organization's work was scandalous was like charging Santa Claus with breaking and entering. We were preparing to play the "pride" card.

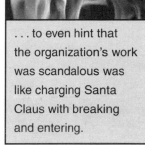

... to even hint that the organization's work was scandalous was like charging Santa Claus with breaking and entering.

The organization's reputation had taken decades of hard work and dedication to build and maintain. Losing that reputation because of allegations made in an anonymous memo was unthinkable.

We knew from the beginning that controlling the release of the allegations was out of our hands. We could only control our reaction to them. Fortunately, the author of the memo was not moving on a particularly fast track. We had been given the gift of at least some time to prepare.

We prepared standby news releases, media statements, and a speech defending the organization. They would be used only if absolutely necessary.

The common theme was that a slap at the organization was a direct insult to every one of the organization's members. Employees, members, and corporate sponsors were lining up in our corner. If this fracas turned into a major battle, the numbers should be on our side.

We wanted to mount an offensive, but we were hesitant to react to charges that at the time only a handful of people knew. We thought about releasing the information ourselves. In that way, we would control the timing, and our side of the story would come out simultaneously, carrying our spin. We decided against it.

Instead, we decided that the company should launch a major goodwill campaign. Speaking engagements, media interviews, and public appearances increased. We took a look at our advertising campaign. We considered carefully every element of communication that we controlled, whether it was newsletters, magazine articles, letters, or email. We wanted to bolster our image as much as possible.

> The organization was willing to spend whatever money was necessary to protect its valuable reputation, which after decades of building was literally priceless.

These communications addressed some of the issues outlined in the accusatory memo. Our message was getting out first, with consistency and to people who needed to hear it.

The organization was willing to spend whatever money was necessary to protect its valuable reputation, which after decades of building was literally priceless. Even if the allegations were never published, the company's actions were hardly a waste of money. We were simply expanding and fine tuning activities we had been doing all along.

Ultimately, portions of the allegations appeared in certain publications. Most of them were elements of bylined columns or opinion pieces. They likely raised a few eyebrows, and some people undoubtedly believed them. The New York reporter to whom the anonymous memo was addressed never followed up on the allegations.

Overall, the attempt to destroy the organization had been stopped in its tracks—at least for the time being.

The reputation of this nonprofit was too powerful and had been built and protected too much over many years for any one disgruntled individual to destroy. The organization's leaders had realized early the potential of what could happen, and they acted immediately. They had a plan and they followed it.

But that organization, like so many others, knows that this particular incursion was just one battle. Attacks against a corporate, organizational, or personal reputation can happen anytime, striking out of nowhere without warning and creating as much damage as any fire or explosion. Attacks on reputations must be dealt with as you would deal with any other crisis. Recognize them for what they are and the danger they present, and be prepared to deal with them.

When Len went to work at his family business one day, he knew there was a problem. His keys wouldn't work. He was locked out of his office. Later, his company car was repossessed. His credit cards were no good. The company his father had started and that Len had grown over the years had effectively fired him. Len was the president of the company, but he was out. His ego was hurt badly. His reputation was soon to be tested.

Len had been a successful businessman over the years: a community and industry leader with the respect of his peers. But when I first met him, I encountered a shadow of what he had once been. "Proud" was not a word I would associate with him on that particular day.

I was reminded of one of those movies placed in the Wild West where the cavalry officer is kicked out of the army in disgrace. They take away his captain's bars, they rip off his insignia, and they break his sword. That type of humiliation summarized the impression I formed of Len that day at the private club where I met him, where he had once entertained friends and big-name customers. He was concerned those days had come to an end.

The breakup of the family business was big news in

Len's hometown. The company was one of the area's leading construction firms, and its workers had built some of the area's most popular landmarks. As the family business grew, the founder's offspring had become voting board members and partial owners. When Len's relatives ended up with more voting rights than his own family, Len wasn't overly concerned. He trusted them, he told me, right up to the day they locked him out of his office. His own relatives had turned against him.

Len had retained lawyers to fight his case. They were optimistic Len would ultimately win. The main question, though, was: what would be left by the time he won his case? Would the victory be hollow?

In round one of the legal action, Len won back his office, but the client base was shaky. The other side of the family had created a new company with a similar name and had already begun grabbing clients. An already dirty fight was growing nastier quickly.

The strategy we were putting together needed a lot more than sound bites. We had already won our first battle on the front page of the newspaper. The main concern now was the survival of the business itself.

The business was more than a half-century old and was showing its age. Upstarts in the industry had picked away at Len's customer base, and the other side of the family was trying to take what was left.

Early on, we had tried to reach customers with the message that Len's firm was "the original" company. We bragged about the company's history and the landmarks the company had built. In addition to concentrating on history, though, I felt we needed to spend more time in the present and concentrate even more on the future. I was moving in this case from crisis management consultant to business, marketing, and design consultant.

We wanted to start touting the "new" company— telling clients we weren't going to simply rest on our laurels. Unfortunately, we still looked like an old company. Len himself looked like a CEO from an era long past. His suits, moustache, and sideburns all placed him in a decade people were trying to forget. His business needed a makeover, as did Len himself.

While a new sign was going up in front of the business, some interior changes were taking place too. Meanwhile, Len was sitting down for an overdue haircut that brought him into the latter part of the 20th century.

The advertising for Len's firm played on its reputation in the industry, but we let people know we were ready for tomorrow. Len's family, employees, friends, and customers were all integral parts of the effort.

> Reputations do not have a strong life of their own. They are fragile. They must be nurtured, protected, and strengthened on a regular basis.

The campaign would be long and difficult. Not only was Len's reputation tarnished when he was locked out of his office, but the reputation of the business he wanted to cling to was tarnished as well. He had counted on the firm's reputation to carry him through the fight and rebuild the business, but the family quarrel and the legal battles had taken their toll. The family business had become damaged goods.

Len had learned the value of a corporate and personal reputation firsthand. His family had spent more than 50 years building the reputation of the company, but only one day was needed to severely damage that reputation. Len would spend a great deal of time, money, and effort rebuilding that reputation over the next several years, but it would still never reach the level where it had once been.

The lesson I learned from my association with Len over the years was that no one should ever take a corporate or personal reputation for granted. Reputations do not have a strong life of their own. They are fragile. They must be nurtured, protected, and strengthened on a regular basis. They are far too valuable to be ignored.

LESSONS LEARNED

A long the way from crisis to crisis, you're bound to learn some valuable lessons. I've certainly learned a few. Some came easy. Others were downright painful.

One of the more painful lessons was when we were asked to conduct a mock disaster for a major hospital. It was pretty straightforward. It would involve all of senior management and many doctors, nurses, managers, and staffers. It was to be realistic. It was to be "believable." The only catch was that the hospital's CEO didn't want participants to know it was a mock disaster.

What developed was a health-care version of "War of the Worlds."

The CEO felt his top executives weren't ready to handle a major crisis. He felt that way, but the top executives did not. He thought they needed some training. His opinion was not shared by his subordinates. He first wanted me to evaluate their media skills without them knowing they were being evaluated.

I hired a local camera crew and went in under the guise that I was a freelance television reporter working on a documentary about the role medical evacuation helicopters had played in saving patients' lives. We were also concerned about the dangers of operating medevac services. I told them I wasn't sure when or where the program would be seen, which was the truth.

Within a matter of a few days, I had interviewed almost every senior-level executive, along with pilots and the people who operated the hospital's helicopter service. It was a good documentary, but it was punctuated throughout with off-the-wall comments that did nothing to instill faith in the safety of the hospital's helicopters.

"It's dangerous," I recall the hospital's chief nurse saying in her interview. "You wouldn't catch me in one of those things."

The next step was to stage the mock disaster. It was scheduled at least three times before we finally pulled the trigger and made it happen. We figured most people at the hospital would see through our charade within 30 minutes tops. We were wrong.

It began about 7 A.M. on a Sunday morning. There was a light plane crash about 50 miles from the hospital, and we dispatched a helicopter to the crash scene. Information would come from the scene via regular channels. Everyone involved in that part of the scenario was alerted to what was going on and all were scripted. As the helicopter was leaving the scene of the accident, it hit a power line and crashed. Our scenario had a substitute pilot and there were no fatalities. In case people would actually believe our story, we wanted to make sure it didn't get overly emotional.

Just to play it safe, we alerted local law enforcement authorities and the FAA that we were staging the drill. They would play along, as necessary.

Within an hour, we had our TV crews at the doorsteps of the hospital. There were phone calls from reporters and from the public. They were all part of our scenario.

It was believable. You might say it was almost too believable.

Word of the "crash" went far beyond the hospital. I just recently learned that a preacher stopped in the middle of his Sunday morning sermon that day for a moment of silence for the victims of the crash. The hospital received one call from a regional television station. How they had heard, I can only guess. Our mock disaster was clearly out of hand.

It continued for two hours before we announced it was a drill. At first, no one believed us. I spent the next two hours going throughout the hospital with the CEO explaining what had happened, and offering our apologies for causing any undue alarm.

We still stage a lot of mock disasters. Most are launched without much warning. We try to make them as realistic as possible. But every single mock disaster since that date has been very clearly labeled a mock disaster.

As far as we were concerned, one War of the Worlds was enough.

Throughout the years, we've coached people for interviews and conducted media training workshops in just about every conceivable venue. Many of them are in state-of-the-art conference centers. Many of them are not.

When you're acting under deadline pressure, you can understand why the training might take place in less-than-desirable surroundings. But when there is enough time to plan and cost is not a major concern, you wonder why anyone would select some of the places they do because the location affects the outcome of the training. It's difficult to take media training seriously when you're being interviewed in a closet. Yes, a closet.

We were at a chemical plant in Illinois with a large company. The room where we conducted the bulk of the training was OK, but there was a problem with the room where we would videotape the interviews. It wasn't available. But there was this adjacent closet. It was barely large enough to accommodate a TV camera, but it was all we had. I doubt very many real interviews are conducted in closets. I hope we don't do any more in closets either. It was Illinois and it was winter, but we soon found out that shooting the interviews outside in the snow was a much better deal. It was better than a closet.

Since that catastrophe, we now try to shoot at least one of our interviews outside, even under poor weather conditions. It's more realistic. And it sure beats conducting interviews in a closet.

We were conducting a workshop for a group of health-care professionals in Biloxi, Mississippi, a few years ago. The training facility was a large building and we had it pretty much to ourselves. Things were looking up. About midway through the workshop, a major rainstorm broke out, accompanied by hail. Our workshop building had a metal roof. You can imagine the rest. We felt we were inside a steel drum.

The chemical company had selected a hotel near the Pittsburgh airport for one class. It was convenient. About an hour into the workshop, planes began leaving the airport in droves. They were flying directly over the hotel. You could wave at the passengers. You could almost feel the tire tracks on the roof before the planes retracted their landing gear. The training was scheduled to continue the entire week. We moved it on Day Two. One day was more than enough at the end of an airport runway.

We were at a relatively new and pretty fancy convention center in Ohio conducting our training when we began hearing a real heavy pounding sound right above the classroom. "It sounds like a herd of elephants up there," complained my associate, Tom Ryan. He went up to investigate. A circus was setting up on the floor above us. That sound was generated by the elephants, Tom discovered.

The conference hotel in Amarillo, Texas, looked like a pretty decent venue. The room was large. The VCR worked. The coffee was OK. Our meeting room was separated from a larger ballroom by one of those plastic accordion walls that can be folded back to create a larger room. I've never seen one of those movable walls that really worked well. This one was no exception.

It was late in the morning and we were rolling along pretty well. They were setting up next door for a meeting of some sort. It wasn't bothering us . . . yet.

Then the motivational speaker came to the podium with a more-than-ample public address system. She was good. The more than 200 nurses in the audience cheered her on, and on . . . and on. We couldn't compete.

On two occasions, we were conducting media training when thunderstorms knocked out electrical power. In one case, we just went over to battery power on the camera and lights and plugged away until the lights came back on. We tried the same approach at a bed and breakfast hotel in Tiffin, Ohio, a couple of years later. The only problem was that the power never came back on. We called another hotel up the road and found the outage was isolated. We picked up the workshop and moved it to the other hotel.

We were conducting our first round of interviews at an office complex near Cincinnati. It was for a chemical company, and the scenario involved a fire and explosion. Firemen were on the scene.

It was exactly then that I looked out the glass wall between our conference room and the front of the building and saw the fire trucks arriving. Firemen began running inside our building. Ultimately, we had to evacuate. There was a real fire.

Then there was the workshop in New Mexico at a country club in a small community. We were utilizing part of what was normally a dance floor. Compared to past experiences, it wasn't bad.

The workers had set up our equipment and I noticed a fork on top of the television set, which was hooked up to a VCR. "I'm sorry," I said, "but I think you missed a fork." He looked back at me and said very clearly. "The fork, sir, is for the VCR. That's how you get the tapes out."

It wasn't particularly an unusual email message, but it was intriguing. It wasn't the kind you automatically trash, and I was pretty sure it didn't contain a virus.

It was from a college student in the United Kingdom. She was a graduate student and she was working on a dissertation on crisis management. She had found us on the Web, and she wanted me to take a few moments to respond to some questions. Unlike so many other requests where students wanted copies of crisis plans or crisis case studies, she wasn't looking for free handouts. She had taken time in developing her questions. She knew what she wanted. Her questions made me think.

She asked: *What type of crisis management strategies do you suggest are the best and why?*

Whew! I had to think about this one. There are so many strategies after all, and what's best for one crisis might not work on another. Then I looked for a common denominator.

I told her that strategies will vary, but they start with determining and understanding the facts, issues, and concerns about the crisis BEFORE trying to come up with a solution on how to handle it. Too often, "would-be" crisis managers seem to know the answer before they know the question. You also need to recognize how the crisis is affecting others and not just your own organization.

Question: *Why do some strategies work while others fail?*

Response: Some fail because they are flawed strategies from the start or they were never implemented correctly. Others fail because no strategy would have worked under the circumstances. Most of the time, strategies fail because they were not well thought out or tested, or the organization failed to take public reaction into the picture. Often, they fail because organizations don't like being told (or forced) into doing the RIGHT thing if they don't believe it needs to be done. And yes, some companies just don't want to spend the money to do what needs to be done.

Question: *What do you think are the biggest mistakes companies make while handling crises?*

Response: There are so many. Where do you want me to start?

They fail to plan. There is no team. There is no crisis plan. There is no strategy. They don't even know they have a crisis until they read about it in the newspaper.

They hold back factual information from those people who are trying to handle the crisis. Companies will entrust someone to handle the company's reputation and potentially its survival, but they won't trust those same people with the facts to get the job done. There is simply no excuse for that.

Another mistake is going into a crisis with blinders on. Crisis managers only see the situation from their own perspective. They operate inside a corporate box with no windows. They fail to put themselves in the public's shoes. Then they wonder why the public is so upset with their actions.

> Crisis management requires teamwork and it requires leadership. Leaders need the skill as well as the authority to get things done.

If preparation is the key to crisis management, why do so many corporations give training such a low priority? You wouldn't want to go to a heart surgeon who had never done surgery before, but corporations entrust the management of crises to untrained individuals. They waste valuable time and make serious mistakes as they are forced to learn crisis management "on the job."

I am continually amazed about the calls we receive from organizations who know they are either in or on the verge of a major crisis and yet don't have the time to deal with it. The future of their company could be going up in smoke, but they can't find the time or resources to plan on how they'll deal with it.

So often, the so-called crisis team is a committee of individuals and no one is really in charge. Crisis management requires teamwork and it requires leadership. Leaders need the skill as well as the authority to get things done.

Another mistake is the lack of commitment to do what is necessary to really resolve the crisis. They know what needs to be done. They're just not willing to do it.

Question: *Have your opinions on the best crisis management strategies changed over the years?*

Response: Yes, but the basics remain the same. Crisis management begins with people, not plans. If you've got the right people, and you make sure they do their homework and then give them the resources, support, and information they need, they'll rarely let you down. The best strategy, sometimes, is to not go into a crisis with a strategy at all, but with an open mind.

Question: *Why do you think some companies are still failing to see the importance of crisis management?*

Response: Perhaps it doesn't relate to the bottom line in their opinion. Others just think they are immune to crisis situations. Why do people still smoke? Why do some people not wear seat belts? They just think they can beat the odds . . . that bad things happen to other people. Or, they think they already have all the answers and they can handle whatever the public and the news media can dish out.

We were working with a food company and the Food and Drug Administration on a food tampering incident in Kansas City a few years ago. The crisis team had been involved for several days, but so far there had been no media calls. That would all change the next day, however. That's when police would arrest a suspect who had already admitted he had contaminated the food.

Once the arrest was made, the tampering would be

public knowledge and we knew we would receive media calls. We wanted to be ready.

I was working with the selected spokesperson in his office and I began going through some mock interviews, asking him the kinds of questions I felt he would get from the media once the arrest was made. We already had a Q&A. We had message points. We knew what we wanted to get across.

At first, the problem was that there were too many "observers" in the room. There were just too many members of the crisis team watching. It made the spokesperson nervous. We kicked all but one of them out. It was better.

The spokesperson had the Q&A and his message points spread out in front of him, but his responses were still not coming out with the kind of natural conviction we wanted.

During a break, I asked one of his colleagues if he could find some flipcharts and a marker. We then wrote our key message points or "nuggets" on the flipchart pads and then tacked those key phrases or responses to questions on the wall in front of the spokesperson's desk.

When the real interviews began later that day, we placed them on a speaker phone so I could hear the questions. They would ask a question and then I'd run over to the preselected "nugget" and point to the answer.

It sounded crazy, but it worked. Our "off-the-wall" answers were in the newspapers the next day.

Despite what you read in the newspapers or see on television, it's pretty difficult to put a good "spin" on a bad news story. Yet, so many corporations think if they hire the right people and pay them enough money, it can be done.

I personally don't think the public is that naive.

Just exactly how do you put a good "spin" on a toxic chemical release that sends dozens of people to the hospital? How do you put a good spin on a hospital mistake that cost a five-year-old child his life?

In a crisis, the truth is almost always certain to come out eventually. I've always felt it was better to put it out yourself rather than wait for someone else to do it for you.

Yet, you'd be surprised how many people are absolutely petrified at the thought of ever admitting their company did something wrong. They're afraid of lawyers, lawsuits, and their career going up in ashes. Yet, time and time again, it seems that organizations that own up to their mistakes fare well in the court of public opinion, if not the legal courts as well. Sometimes, the best crisis strategy is to simply apologize.

> Time and time again, it seems that organizations that own up to their mistakes fare well in the court of public opinion, if not the legal courts as well. Sometimes, the best crisis strategy is to simply apologize.

If you're looking for a crisis management consultant to help you in an emergency, the "yellow pages" is probably not the best place to turn. It's not that there's anything wrong with the yellow pages; it's just by that time, it's a little late to start shopping around.

Yet, that's exactly what happens in many crises. The company waits until the crisis is at a full burn before they start looking for any outside assistance. And even though they have the possibility of watching their business crash and burn, they want to see references and quibble over fees and expenses. Often, they won't even consider working on a weekend or holiday or think about juggling their own schedule to handle a crisis.

Crises are difficult enough to handle when everything works right. If you can't or are unwilling to devote the time and resources necessary, you're almost certainly doomed to failure.

The best time to figure out how your organization can handle a crisis is before the crisis ever takes place. That's the time to research and find potential outside resources. It's a much better time to find out about qualifications, experience, fees, and availability. You can look in directories or on the Internet, but you'll also want to check with others you know and trust.

It's sort of like looking for a good doctor or lawyer. If you're looking for someone to help you out in a crisis, ask others whom they've used and if they'd recommend that firm to others.

WHERE DO WE
GO FROM HERE?

A s I write this, I'm in the Delta Air Lines Crown Room
at the Greater Cincinnati/Northern Kentucky Airport. It is January 3, 2002, and I'm on my way to a very
delayed flight to Dallas, Texas.

The news on the television in the lounge is all about
the war in Afghanistan and the Rose Bowl. Passengers
are divided: 90 percent want to watch the game. I want
to watch the news. As a native of Indiana and now a resident of Columbus and the home of The Ohio State University, I am not totally excited about a game being
played two days late and with no meaning to the Big 10.
I'd rather watch the latest developments on the other
side of the world. My interest at the moment is whether
my delayed flight—originally scheduled to leave at

5 P.M.—will make it at 11:30 P.M., or will I have to wait until tomorrow's 9 A.M. flight. Whatever happens, it's OK with my client. I've already called them and they know the snowstorm in Atlanta has created havoc for just about everyone traveling this particular day.

The trip started out more than 24 hours ago. I was still recuperating from New Year's Eve when the pager gave us a garbled message about 5:30 P.M. on January 2. I figured it was another one of those messages intended for someone else. I was wrong.

When we called our message service to interpret what the message was all about, we found out it was urgent. We needed to do something right away. How soon could we be in Dallas?

Is this a slow-burning crisis? Or is this one that will explode quickly? At this time, no one knows. We just know we have to get ready.

Thanks to weather delays, I've had ample opportunities to prepare. I've already thought about possible questions and message points, even though I'm not sure yet what the issues are.

Can they be that different from other issues of this kind, I keep asking myself? I don't know. I just know I want to go into tomorrow morning's meeting with some ideas. That's why they asked me to join them. I want to be as prepared as I can be. What can I do? How can I prepare myself?

I begin looking back at previous cases that were similar to what I think we're looking at now. Can it apply here? Who knows? Regardless, I'm recalling message points, questions and responses, and potential strategies. I'm already thinking about who would make the best spokesperson, even though I've yet to meet the potential candidates.

It is now 11:30 P.M. EST and the time posted for my flight to Dallas is 2:30 A.M. Will it ever take off, or are the airlines just trying to get off an ugly joke? I'm thinking seriously of switching over to American Airlines on my next trip to Dallas.

My videographer is taking a well-deserved catnap. We've been on the road for almost 12 hours and we've flown just 116 miles. We still have 812 miles to go. If all goes well, we'll get into the hotel no later than 4:30 A.M.

Now, once again, why is it I chose to become a crisis management consultant? Was it the glamour? I don't think so. How about the travel? Well, Cincinnati is a great place, but after 10 hours, I've seen about as much of its airport as I want to.

As we were driving to the airport this afternoon, I told my wife that while I could think of other things I'd rather be doing at that particular moment, there was a degree of pride in trying to make the best of bad situations, especially when you're successful. It's always a challenge, but it's one of those challenges you want to accept.

Meanwhile, as we waited to see if the pilot from La Guardia would finally show up and fly our plane to Dallas, my videographer was sleeping—or at least trying to sleep in that blue plastic thing outside Gate B-10 that resembles a chair. He didn't seem to care anymore. He was numb. It was just another assignment to him. In his 10 years with me, it was just another job, perhaps a boring job at the time. Hanging around airports and waiting on rental cars had taken its toll. Now, it was just a matter of what we could do to help out a client. Perhaps, just perhaps, we might be able to help them out. Perhaps, if we ever get there.

Although the events of September 11, 2001, stopped our business in its tracks as it did most other businesses in the United States, the lull was only temporary. Shortly afterward, there was a newfound interest in crisis management across the country.

Prompted, perhaps, by a realization that the impossible is now frighteningly possible, more and more businesses began taking a serious look at how they could survive a major crisis, or avoid one.

They know the odds of a plane crashing into their corporate headquarters, hospital, nuclear facility, or chemical plant is highly unlikely, but they know all too well that it can happen. It already has.

They are taking off their corporate blinders and they are thinking: "Perhaps, just perhaps, it could happen to us."

They know that while terrorist attacks are now a reality in America, it doesn't have to be a terrorist attack. It can be a disgruntled employee. It can be an accident. It can just be a case of bad luck.

And fortunately, they are doing more than just thinking about it. They're engaging in training programs and emergency drills. They are looking at the endless list of possibilities that could impact their operations, and they're trying to make sure they are prepared.

To a much lesser degree, that has been the case following other disasters and crises. Following a crisis that affects a major food company, other companies suddenly want to examine their crisis plans and make sure they're not vulnerable to the same kind of event.

When an explosion rocks a chemical plant in France, chemical companies around the world take a closer look at how they could handle such a catastrophe.

Unfortunately, that air of concern—that need to do something to protect one's self—usually doesn't last that long. Once the event that prompted the concern is no longer on the evening news or the front page of the newspaper, crisis management begins to become less and less a major priority.

In the overall scope of business management, that's dangerous.

Even when the event that prompted the concern is no longer making headlines, the potential for another event has not necessarily ended.

There's one thing I'm certain about after working in the field of crisis management for the past 15 years. I'm certain it is not a question of "if" a crisis will take place, but simply when.

POSTSCRIPT

The book was already finished and in the publisher's hands when I returned to Oklahoma City for another crisis management seminar. To my surprise, one of my students was the same man who had inspired me to write this book on an earlier visit to Oklahoma City. He's the one who told me my course probably hadn't prepared him to appear on *60 Minutes*, but at least he wouldn't "step in it" if interviewed by reporters.

I talked to him briefly, and he told me how he still didn't like the idea of doing on-camera interviews. He was still apprehensive about dealing with reporters during anything that even closely resembled a crisis. Yet, he was there.

He was taking the course, and his job, very seriously, I thought.

His first interview was pretty good. He was all business.

As the day progressed, he became better and better.

During one of the breaks, I told him about the book and how his comments had been an inspiration to me. By the end of the day, his interviews and comments were an inspiration to everyone there.

ACKNOWLEDGMENTS

So many people were instrumental in prompting me to write this book—and helping me write this book—that there is no way I can mention all of them.

There are the clients—and in many cases close friends who happen to be clients—who have urged me for years to put together a book on our crisis management endeavors. They are also the people who gave me the material on which this book is based. They've allowed me to enjoy what I feel might just be the best job in the world. Without them, there would be no book.

There is Tom Ryan, my longtime associate and very close friend who has urged me to write this book for at least a decade or more. He also provided some of the material, along with any humor the book contains. He was also with me during so many of those road trips for media training workshops and mock disasters from Boston to San Diego and scores of communities in between.

There are all those other associates I've had the honor to work with who've shared their experience, skills, and talent to help us tame those impossible crises and carry out those realistic scenarios.

There is my wife, Donna, who encouraged me to get into the business of crisis management. She's put up with my travel schedule and crazy work schedule, both as a wife and as a business associate. Without her, the book would never have been possible.

And I'd like to offer a special thanks to my former editor at *The Cincinnati Enquirer*, Luke Feck. If it weren't for Luke, I'm not sure I would have ever become a political reporter, let alone a crisis management consultant.

Luke is one of those people who demands the best of you. He doesn't settle for anything less.

Finally, there is my son, Jeff. He not only kept harassing me to write the book, but he helped me write it. Many of the scenarios, the ideas, the thoughts, were his. He was clearly the motivation factor.

ABOUT THE AUTHOR

S teve Wilson learned about crisis management the hard way shortly after
graduating from high school. He was
working on a farm in Rush County, Indiana, when he managed to wreck the boss's
tractor and found himself unemployed and
forced to find a new line of work. His job
search ended when he found an opening
for a reporter at a weekly newspaper near
Indianapolis. The job didn't pay much, it
had long hours, but it sounded interesting
and there were no tractors involved.

That was the launch of a career in journalism that later
took him to Vietnam, where he served as a U.S. Army
combat correspondent, and later to the campaign trails of
American politics. He served as a political reporter for
The Cincinnati Enquirer and won one of the nation's top
awards for business and economic reporting while a reporter for Gannett News Service. He later joined the staff
of *USA Today* and was chief of its Chicago news bureau.

He eventually traded in his press card for a career in
public relations, and in 1987, he launched Wilson Group
Communications, a consulting firm specializing solely in
crisis management communications and media training.

His consulting work has taken him to nearly every
U.S. state, as well as Canada and Mexico. Each year, he

conducts more than 100 workshops and seminars across the United States and has lectured on crisis management at various universities and for professional associations. He's authored scores of articles on crisis management and media response training for magazines and newspapers and has been interviewed as a crisis management specialist for publications ranging from *Modern Healthcare* to the *Wall Street Journal*.

FOR MORE INFORMATION ON
THE WILSON GROUP:

Web: www.wilson-group.com

Email: info@wilson-group.com

Phone: 800-313-9424